Coached by

Christ

**Living
a new kind
of life**

Coached by
Christ

Living
a new kind
of life

Andy Peck

Published 2005 by CWR, Waverley Abbey House, Waverley Lane, Farnham, Surrey GU9 8EP, England.

See back of book for list of National Distributors.

Unless otherwise indicated, all Scripture references are from the Holy Bible: New International Version (NIV), copyright © 1973, 1978, 1984 by the International Bible Society.
RSV: Revised Standard Version © 1965, Division of Christian Education of the National Council of the Churches of Christ in the United States of America.

Front cover image: Getty Images/Time and Life Pictures: Ed Clark

Concept development, editing, design and production by CWR

Printed in Finland by WS Bookwell

ISBN 1-85345-348-X

Contents

Introduction

The theologian, Karl Barth, was asked to sum up what he had learnt as a theologian. He replied in the words of a children's chorus: 'Jesus loves me, this I know, for the Bible tells me so.'

At one level Christianity is delightfully simple, even a child can understand. But working out what Christianity means for us in daily life is not so easy.

- Maybe you take your faith seriously but aren't sure what to do to make progress. Discipleship programmes haven't brought the development you had hoped for. You begin to wonder whether you are a true Christian at all.
- You have become discouraged that you can't meet the high demands of Scripture. You fake it when you are with other Christians, but know deep down that you aren't growing in love for God and your neighbour the way you would like.
- Other Christians seem to have a hot-line to God. You become puzzled, where others seem to have such certainty. Why?
- Maybe you are not yet a Christian and are puzzled about Christianity. You are not sure what to make of church and aren't sure what would be expected of you. You suspect you wouldn't match up.

Help is at hand. Jesus tells us what to expect and how to live. Our problem is that we have neglected His teaching, or failed to realise how it applies to us. You can be 'coached by Christ' if you will learn from the way He coached the Twelve and others who followed Him when He was on earth. He is prepared to work with you, if you will only let Him.

Reading a book on improving the Christian life is a scary business. It's scary because you know it may be costly, and aren't sure how God may challenge you, whether you are a Christian or not. It's a fair assumption that things will need to change, and you may not like it. But remember, the cost of not following Christ is actually far higher than doing so; it won't seem like a cost when you really understand what the Christian life is and how it works – it's totally liberating. You won't look back.

Why this book?

In four years as a student worker with UCCF and as a pastor/Bible teacher at three churches in the south of England, I have observed first hand different models of Christian growth. Some I have tried and rejected, some I didn't think would help, some promised much but failed to deliver. More recently, five years with *Christianity* magazine have exposed me to a variety of methods and claims of success in the UK and worldwide. I have had to ask, who is right? what works?

My greatest advance in understanding came by reading and listening to Dallas Willard, Professor of Philosophy at University of California. In a conference in London in 2002, I heard Willard say that he knew of no church in North America that helps people 'do' the teaching of Jesus. As I reflected on this, I thought that this may be true for the UK, too, and decided to ask what it would be like to focus on the way Jesus taught His followers as a way of teaching spiritual growth. I read the four Gospels and realised that the modern concept of coaching has parallels with the way Christ coached the Twelve and those who followed Him. I identified 180-plus occasions where Jesus tells us 'to do'. I then grouped the verses under the themes you find in the chapter headings. The book is not exhaustive, but I have identified the major areas we need to grasp.

Inevitably, our understanding of Christ's coaching of the Twelve is informed by the way the rest of the New Testament speaks of spiritual growth. Nevertheless, for the purposes of this book I have looked at how the Twelve were coached by Christ, rather than how the other New Testament writers understood this theme. I am not ignoring the fact that God has included another 23 books in the New Testament, nor that the Twelve occupy a unique period in salvation history. They were Christ-followers, but not yet indwelt by the Spirit. Scholars argue about when they 'came to faith' and the extent to which they are an appropriate model for us. But both John and Matthew explicitly state that the content of their Gospels was intended to equip people who follow Jesus. Matthew quotes Jesus' command that the apostles make disciples by teaching them to obey all that He had commanded them and John says that his Gospel was written that the readers might believe (literally 'go on believing'). The apostles consciously penned their Gospels in order that we would know what Jesus intends. Our situation as people who benefit from Christ's death, resurrection, ascension and gift of the Spirit may be different, but Jesus' teaching is still for us today as powerful as for the Twelve.

How it is arranged

The book is arranged into 30 chapters to encourage readers to consider carefully each element before moving on. Some may choose to read it as 30 daily studies. Action points are included as a reminder that we are to 'do' what Jesus commanded, not read about it in a book.

In Part One we see that our Christian life is based on the life and teaching of Christ, nothing else. We need to be sure of His good intentions for us, how He works with us and why He is the model for our living what I have called the 'new kind of life'.

Part Two takes us through what must be fundamental thinking regarding sin, the work of the Holy Spirit, our new relationship through Christ to the Law of God, and the imperative role of talking with our Coach as we learn from Him how to be like Him.

Part Three could be the most crucial section of all. Our transformation involves the totality of our lives, so that we become like Christ from the inside out: in our thinking, our feeling, our choosing, our body and our soul.

Part Four explores how the new kind of life shows itself in and through our relationships. We can't claim to love God whom we have not seen if we don't love our neighbour whom we have.

Part Five focuses upon how we impact our world for Christ, knowing His life and power, to make a difference in communities wherever we are based. Nothing can hinder us from this task and if we never practise Part Five, we have failed to grasp what being coached by Christ is about.

Part Six closes with a look at the life to come, both within and beyond this earth-based life.

PART ONE

Meet the Coach

The first section of the book is foundational to all that follows. Christians first need to appreciate what Christ has called them to. Is Christianity about creeds and behaviour plans, or is there more to it? In what sense is He my coach? How do my aspirations for change fit in with those of Jesus?

And despite the fact that Jesus is no stranger to us, we need to be sure that we follow the Jesus of the Bible and not one cobbled together by half-truth and hearsay. Why should I trust Him, and what does becoming like Him mean in the twenty-first century?

CHAPTER 1

Jesus is in the coaching business

Watching myself on video is no fun, especially when I am trying my hardest to play a game I love. Watching the tape that recorded my best attempts at hitting a golf ball made me want to throw my clubs away altogether. A golfing pro had opened a Teaching Centre just 50 yards from where I was working in Bournemouth and I figured the five-session special offer of £65 was just what I required if my golf game was to become half decent.

Teaching Centre was a grand name for what was actually a converted shop. It had a golf mat, golf net and a video camera that faced the player. The golfing pro, an Irishman with a keen wit, promised me that he had helped worse cases than me. I wasn't sure whether to be encouraged or not.

Using a 7-iron golf club, my swing was videoed so that the pro could replay my attempts at launching the ball, and explain why my intentions and my execution were so far apart. The filming of the whole lesson, which was supposed to help, was deeply discouraging; in my mind I hit the ball with the smoothness of a tournament pro, the video actually reminded me of a farmer with a scythe at harvest time. But I persevered; I had parted with £65 after all, and over the five sessions, the pro got to work. He changed my grip, stance, takeaway and initial movement back to the ball – ie pretty well everything. By the end of five sessions I knew what I had been doing wrong, how I could correct it and what I needed to practise if I were to resemble the photographs of some of the tournament pros that covered the wall of the former shop. In spite of the embarrassment, this was a coach who knew his stuff and, more importantly, could convey that knowledge in such a way that I could change.

Imagine if spiritual growth could be handled the same way. Someone videos our life, gives us feedback and ways to improve. Would we make faster progress? Or would we be too scared even to start?

When we look at the New Testament, we see a coach at work. Being a disciple in Jesus' time meant being coached or trained by the person you were joined with – learning skills and imitating the way of life of the master. The Twelve were to learn from Jesus how to live like Him 24/7, observing His life, hearing His stupendous teaching, watching His extraordinary miracles, and becoming involved themselves in seeing radical changes in people's lives.

This coaching was the model on which coaching of future followers would be based. Before He left earth He told His disciples: 'All authority in heaven and on earth has been given to me. Therefore go and make disciples of all nations, baptising them in the name of the Father and of the Son and of the Holy Spirit, and teaching them to obey everything I have commanded you. And surely I am with you always, to the very end of the age' (Matt. 28:18–19). The coaching involved teaching – in groups and one to one – and the sort of close observation I received from the golf pro.

Christianity has become so divorced from the life of the first-century disciples that it is possible to live as a Christian today with little or no knowledge of how Jesus intends us to live, yet He urged His first followers to 'make disciples' specifically by teaching people to obey what He had commanded. Some may want the benefits of relationship with God without looking to change, but my experience of travelling around student groups for four years and working as a pastor and Bible teacher, suggests that even Christians who are half-hearted about their faith want to grow, if only they knew how. They want to deal with traits within their own character, they want to be more effective in helping friends and family, they want to know the closeness to God that they see others enjoy.

The author of *Christian Coaching*, Gary Collins, defines coaching as 'the art and practice of guiding a person or group from where they are toward a greater competence and fulfilment that they desire'.[1]

Jesus is still in the coaching business and offers us the same specialist help that He gave the Twelve. By His Spirit He will help you change so that you enjoy the life He has for you. He's seen the video of your life. He's identified the flaws and rejoiced in the successes. He's not out to embarrass you, He just wants to know when you want to get serious about it.

What Jesus didn't say

Jesus' coaching does not imitate the model of the less prescriptive styles of coaching today which aim to draw the answers from the client. Jesus' coaching is most definitely prescriptive. We know we don't have the answers within ourselves and are only too glad that He teaches us.

Furthermore, many models of Christian growth have been popular throughout the history of the Church but have depended more on our discipline than God's work. Being coached by Christ is not the spiritual equivalent of training for a marathon, where the coach gives you new exercises and schedules which you gradually build up in readiness for the day when you run. It is not a case of try harder, do more, learn more, as if it's all about 'upping the spiritual tempo'. Such spiritual growth methods leave the practitioners proud of what they have achieved, leave the dropouts perpetually guilty and the leaders wondering why life is being sucked out of the believers. You cannot live the Christian life by direct effort. Being coached by Christ means that we are trained so that we will naturally live the life He calls us to. It will take the gracious resources of God and effort on our part, but we won't feel as though we are on a permanent marathon schedule. Who'd want to live like that?

Main points

- Jesus intends us to become like Him.
- The coach–coachee model that operated with Christ's 12

disciples is still in operation today.
- You need to accept His advice.

ACTION

1. Tell Jesus that you are pleased that He is your Coach. Ask Him to isolate those areas where He wants you to grow.
2. Make a decision to be intentional about your growth from now on, using this book, the insights of other Christians and time reflecting in prayer, to follow the agenda that Jesus has for you.
3. Set aside time with Him each day. Even a short time is better than no time.

Note

1. Gary R Collins, *Christian Coaching* (Navpress 2001).

Chapter 2

You are welcomed to a new kind of life

Every coach has a goal. He might be asked to increase an athlete's speed or improve a client's interviewing skill. She might be asked to revolutionise a manager's ability to mentor others, or identify why an executive is slow to make decisions. What about Jesus? What would you imagine His goal might be for you? To deal with a particular sin you are tempted to commit? To stay out of trouble? To convert your family? To become a missionary?

Jesus summarised His coaching purpose like this: 'I have come that they may have life, and have it to the full' (John 10:10).

He aims that we enter into and enjoy a new kind of life.

Jesus spent the majority of His three-year ministry travelling around the Galilee region of first-century Palestine. At the heart of His teaching was this call to a new kind of life. He was inviting people to learn from Him how to live in friendship with God.

The four Gospel writers describe it in different but complementary ways. Matthew writes of us entering the kingdom of heaven. Mark and Luke call it entering the kingdom of God, John prefers receiving 'eternal life'. They all mean similar things. The word 'kingdom' speaks of the place where what God wants done is done. John's use of 'eternal' reminds us that this new life is of a special quality that continues beyond death. My expression 'a new kind of life' attempts to sum up all three expressions.

What is the life?

John describes it as eternal life and records the only outright definition of this life anywhere in the New Testament. In Jesus' prayer in front of His disciples, He says: 'Now this is eternal life: that they may know you, the only true God, and Jesus Christ, whom you have sent' (John 17:3). 'To know' in the Bible invariably means a relationship of intimacy, so this new life comes to us through a relationship with Jesus and His Father; via the new birth as God's Spirit enables us to respond to Christ's invitation to learn what this new kind of life is like.

We need to be very clear at this point. Jesus never divorced trusting Him for life *after* death from trusting Him for life *before* death. Christianity is not an insurance policy that provides us with 'heaven' when we die, providing we make the weekly payments of church and Bible reading. The Christianity Jesus brings is life in the kingdom of God which is lived now and continues beyond death. It was this life that He was offering His hearers and it is this life He still offers us today. Every day the Twelve observed Jesus living life in close company with God His Father. Every day He invited them to join Him in living under God's rule and reign so that their lives would be a place where 'what God wants done is done'.

Jesus didn't just provide the Twelve with an assurance that all would be OK when they died and then move on to another group. This was ongoing training, to last three years, while He was physically present, and beyond as His Spirit worked with them. It was in listening to His words and acting on them that they would discover what living with Him in the kingdom was about. This was to be the model that He would use with everyone who put their confidence in Him.

This new kind of life has been given to every believer without exception. Our understanding and appreciation of it grows as we learn from Jesus how to live as He did in a process that will continue for the rest of our lives. We allow Him to coach us so that we are changed from the inside out, that all the benefits of knowing God and living by the power of God can become second nature to us.

Many believers know this to be true in theory, but find it doesn't work out in practice. Why is it our life feels like nothing has changed at all? The answer to that question is worked out in the chapters of this book. But for now an illustration may help. When we become Christians we are like a house that is re-wired with the new life. We can welcome the 'power' to the rooms of our life, or we can restrict it, or even shut the rooms off altogether. In some cases we are so ignorant of the sort of life that we are called to live that we have no vision for it, and accept religious substitutes instead. Our life is 're-wired', but we bring in battery-operated appliances that we hope will satisfy us – money, friends, reputation, for example. The living of the new kind of life requires our co-operation, to use the power wired into us and not settle for substitute sources of power that will not truly satisfy us. It is quite possible for us to be a Christian but live in the dark because we are not harnessing the potential within us. Sound familiar? Christ is at work by His Spirit to encourage us to turn the lights on in all aspects of life: in our home, our neighbourhood, our workplace, our leisure pursuits, among our family, our friends, our colleagues, our enemies. The light comes on when we obey His Word in these arenas and allow God's reign to be seen and known. That level of coaching may sound very extreme. Can we imagine ourselves having the compassion of Jesus for people who mistreat us, the love of Jesus for people we don't think deserve love, the peace of Jesus when chaos is all around, the joy of Jesus when life is humdrum?

A grid showing the contrast between our old life and the new life will help us get a handle on the two worlds

	Entrance	Influence	Evidence	Final outcome
Old life	Natural birth	Parents, friends, culture.	Largely self-focused living	Separation from God eternally
New kind of life	New birth when we respond to the call of Christ	Parents, friends, culture. Word of God, Spirit of God, people of God	Growing likeness to Christ as we are changed from the inside out	New life continues with bodies fitted for the world to come

Developing the new kind of life

Jill comes to faith at the age of 17. She is deeply sorry for the way she has lived up to this point, recognises that her sins are great in God's sight and that she needs God's mercy. She asks that Jesus' death would count for her, acknowledging that Jesus died the death she deserved to die. She asks for forgiveness and help to live the new kind of life that God promises. At this point, she enters the new kind of life. It is a life that God's Spirit has encouraged her to seek and find. Now that same Spirit lives within her and encourages her to live a life pleasing to God. However, although everything is in place for growth to take place, Jill has to co-operate.

There is an overlap between the old and new life. Her memory isn't wiped. Her mind is still prey to anxious thoughts. She is still focused on earning pots of money and buying a fast car. She is still envious of girls who have boyfriends. Her life has the potential for growth, but unless she works to change, it won't happen. She can stifle the Spirit's work or refuse to recognise that Jesus understands what needs to happen for her to change.

Acknowledging that there is an old life–new life struggle must not diminish our vision for what God can do in us. Many assume that kingdom living is for the super saints of the Bible. They can imagine Abraham, Moses and the apostle Paul living a 'new kind of life', but not them. For years I had incorrectly understood that being 'saved' was primarily a future deal – change in my present behaviour was an optional extra. But these men do not have any spiritual advantages over me. They may have been anointed to accomplish things that have a greater impact on the world, but God will not hold out on me from knowing the same life they knew and He won't hold out on you either. Growth is possible as we become apprentices in a lifelong calling to follow Christ. We won't live the perfect life He lived, but we can still aim high. He won't settle for anything less.

WHAT JESUS DIDN'T SAY

Jesus never promised a shortcut to becoming like Him. There may be times in our life when we sense a greater energy for God. It may feel as though we have moved into another plane of spiritual experience and can identify a conference, a prayer, a book or a conversation that moved us on. That's great. But nothing replaces the need for us to 'follow Christ' tomorrow. Coached by Christ is a lifelong deal. There are no certificates of merit. We can know that Christ won't let us go and has the prize of glory awaiting us, but until then we press on.

MAIN POINTS

- Jesus' aim is that you enter into and enjoy the new kind of life.
- This life centres on putting your confidence in Him to teach you how to live.
- As you expand your vision of what God can do and consciously involve Him in your life, you will change.

ACTION

1. Remind yourself that no other believer has any advantage over you.
2. Take it as read that God intends great things for you. Write it somewhere so you can remind yourself daily.
3. This new kind of life is yours, but you may need to try it out more than you do. Talk to the Coach about ways in which the new kind of life isn't known in your life, and do what He tells you.

Chapter 3

No one taught like this man

I thought I had said goodbye to exams in 1986, having completed five years of continuous higher education. But here I was facing exams again, 13 years later. I had enrolled on a 14-week Higher National Diploma in journalism and was facing a pretty daunting shorthand exam. It was one of just two exams we had to pass to complete the course, 95 per cent of it was approved course work. Every morning of the 14 weeks was devoted to shorthand as we aimed for a pass mark of 80 words a minute. The exam was simple: the tutor would read a series of scripts, lasting around a minute. We would take shorthand notes of the text, and then decipher the notes afterwards. The scripts would become progressively faster: 50 words a minute; 60 words a minute etc. By the time the tutor reached 100 words a minute, most of us had dropped out of even attempting to take notes. The week before the exam I had reached a level when I was confident I could do 60 words a minute, 70 occasionally. But the pass mark was 80.

I can still remember the moment when the tutor began what seemed to be a normal morning of shorthand practice with an announcement: 'You will be interested to know that the pass mark for the shorthand exam is actually 60. It was always 60 but I said it was 80 because with a lower target, you wouldn't have tried hard enough!' Knowing I could do 60 even on a bad day I felt instant relief – I was sure to pass. But the warm feelings didn't last long – all the effort of 13 weeks had been focused on a lie because she thought that we wouldn't do our best to be as fast as possible. To her, the ends justified the means, but for most of us it left a bad taste

How Christ coaches you

We have seen already that Christ is coaching us to become like Him by inviting us to enter and enjoy a new kind of life. His invitation to do this is clear. Whatever we may have felt about the Christian life up to this point, this is His invitation. He is straight with us about what He expects, where He is leading us and how we will succeed. If you read through the Gospels, Matthew and John especially, you discover that the coaching of the Twelve involved a lot of teaching. Jesus taught His selected twelve 'apostles' (literally 'sent ones'), the 70 (a larger gathering who shared His ministry), and those that gathered to hear Him, whoever they were, wherever they came from. If your school felt like a prison, you may struggle to feel positive about anyone's teaching but it really was the case that, 'No-one ever spoke the way this man does' (John 7:46). Crowds flocked to hear Him. Most of Jesus' teaching was to a group He selected. At the time Jesus grew up, some ordinary members of the public would choose which Jewish teacher (rabbi) they wanted to learn from and imitate. It was unheard of for the 'rabbi' to select those he wanted to follow him, but Jesus handpicked those who He wanted to train. If you are a Christian, the Bible is clear that it is no accident. Jesus has handpicked you, too, and intends to coach you through His teaching, and your response.

Secondly, His teaching was linked with activity. The disciples were not taken through a strict curriculum, but also learned as they observed the way Christ lived. When the Gospels announce that Jesus was calling the Twelve, we are told that they were to be with Him 'to preach, heal and cast out demons' (Matt. 10:1; Mark 3:14). As you view your world and its joys and pain, Christ will coach you to make a difference there.

Thirdly, His teaching was part of His overall mission to model a kind of life that His apprentices would take on when He had gone. He is travelling around, but has one eye on His final rendezvous with a cross in Jerusalem. So there's an urgency about His words, He's in a battle, one He knows He'll win, but a real one nevertheless. This is the teaching of a general marshalling his troops, or a coach training up his fellow players to compete successfully in the game of life.

Jesus didn't teach formally, like a platform speaker at a conference who disappears after the talk is over; He interacted with the Twelve every day and explained in more detail what they had witnessed, or how they could better understand His words. So after the 'feeding of the five thousand' miracle He asked whether they understood what the miracle was about (Mark 8:17). At Caesarea Philippi He asked the Twelve to tell Him what the opinion polls were saying about who He was, and then, who *they* thought He was (Matt. 16:15).

The words of Jesus form a key part of our coaching today. It was His words to you, however they came, that caused you to respond. His words tell you what the new kind of life is like, how you can live it, how you can help others know it, why you struggle, and what to do about it. Nothing's barred. Nothing's too small. He calls you to an ongoing conversation about life.

At first we think the coaching is not the same as if He were physically present and observing our life; after all He can't say, 'When you relate to that person you act defensively, have you noticed?' But as His Spirit applies the Word to us and we speak to Him, it is possible for Him to coach us in the details. And He has placed us in a community where, if the community works, people can help us understand ways in which we can improve.

So the setting for your coaching is exactly where you are now. You don't need to change a thing. He will coach you with your family, your friends, at home, at school, at college, at the club, in your leisure pursuits. Of course, He may ask you to adjust things, but don't think that anything you do is not of interest. This book will give you some clues about what He says, but read the Gospels for yourself and get some insights first hand. Treasure you dig yourself is precious, and with God's Word, it is definitely 'finders keepers'.

What He says to you

When I read through the Gospels, I was able to identify 180 specific commands that Jesus gives. (No doubt there are more.)

I have roughly divided them into themes. Most are covered somewhere in this book.

A new kind of life with God

Love God with all your heart and soul
and mind and strength (Matt. 22:37; Mark 12:30).
Love God (Luke 11:42).
Believe God (John 1:12).
Receive the Holy Spirit (John 20:22).
Don't blaspheme against the Holy Spirit (Mark 3:29).
Have faith in God (Matt. 17:20; Mark 11:22; Luke 17:6).
Don't test God (Luke 4:12).
Worship God alone (Luke 4:8).

A new kind of life with Jesus

Follow Him (Mark 1:17; 10:21; Luke 5:11).
'Hate' family, to follow (Luke 14:26).
Forsake all, to follow (Luke 14:33).
Don't be ashamed of following (Luke 7:23).
Deny self, take up the cross (Matt. 16:24).
Belief as Son of God (Luke 10:22).
Believe in Jesus (John 3:16; 6:29; 10:42; 12:44; 14:1; 14:11;
    20:29).
Ask in His name (John 14:13).
Remain in Jesus (John 15:4).
Don't love family more than Jesus (Matt. 10:35–37).
Eat His body and drink His blood? (John 6:53).
Enter by the gate [Jesus] (John 10:9).
Believe the words of Jesus (John 10:42).
Believe in the resurrection (John 11:25).
Don't reject Jesus (John 12:48).
Trust Jesus as the way, the truth and the life (John 14:6).
Enter by Jesus (Matt. 7:14).

A new life in conversation with Jesus and His Father

If you have faith you can move mountains (Matt. 17:20).

Watch and pray (Matt. 26:41; Luke 21:36).

Pray in secret (Matt. 6:6).

The Lord's Prayer (Matt. 6:9–13; Luke 11:2–4).

Believing prayer (Matt. 21:22).

Pray not to be tempted (Luke 22:46).

Ask in Jesus' name (John 14:13).

Fast happily (Matt. 6:17).

Believe in your heart and ask in prayer (Mark 11:22).

Consider nature (Luke 12:23ff.).

The new kind of life

Seek the kingdom first (Matt. 6:33).

Enter the narrow gate (Luke 13:24).

Everyone's welcome in the kingdom (Matt. 5:3–10).

Repent for the kingdom is at hand (Matt. 4:17; Mark 1:15).

A new kind of life with others

Love others (John 13:34).

Love one another (John 13:34; 15:17).

Wash others' feet (John 13:14).

Do to others as you would have them do to you (Luke 6:31).

Be slave of all (Matt. 20:26).

Forgive others' sins (Matt. 18:21–22).

Reconcile (Matt. 5:24).

Bless those who curse you (Luke 6:28).

Don't judge (Luke 6:37).

'Hate' your family, to follow (Luke 14:26).

Don't discriminate (Matt. 13:30).

Beware of false prophets (Matt. 7:15).

A new kind of life in the world

Let your light shine (Matt. 5:16).
Confess Jesus before men (Matt. 10:32).
Don't fear persecution (Matt. 5:12).
Make disciples (Matt. 28:19).
Don't deny Jesus (Matt. 26:31).
Don't have religious titles (Matt. 23:9).
Don't show off (Matt. 23:5).

A new sensitivity to sin

Sort out the heart (Luke 11:35).
Don't worry (Luke 12:2).
Repent (Luke 13:5).
Rejoice over sinners repenting (Luke 15:32).
Don't cause others to sin (Luke 17:1).
Don't practise sin (Mark 7:23).
Avoid behaviour of the Pharisees and Herodians (Mark 8:15).
Don't lust (Matt. 5:28).
Don't divorce unjustly (Matt. 5:32; Mark 10:11).
Don't think uncleanness is just external (Mark 7:14–15)
Forgive from the heart (Matt. 6:14; 18:35).
Make sure heart and lips match (Matt. 15:8–9).
Be perfect (Matt. 5:48).
Make sure your righteousness exceeds that of Pharisees
    and scribes (Matt. 5:20).
Don't swear (Matt. 5:34).
Don't be angry (Matt. 5:22).
Don't be contemptuous (Matt. 5:22).
Deny self (Matt. 16:24).
Don't cause others to stumble (Matt. 18:6).
Avoid sin (Matt. 18:9).
Don't love life (John 12:25).
Don't desire to be great (Mark 10:44).

A new attitude to resources

Do not serve God and money (Matt. 6:24).
Do not lay up treasures on earth (Matt. 6:19).
Don't idolise your possessions (Luke 18:22).
Do not covet (Luke 12:15).
Do acts of charity secretly (Matt. 6:1).
Receive 100-fold (Mark 4:20).
Don't labour for food that spoils (John 6:27).

A new authority in life

Do and teach the Word (Matt. 5:19).
Hear and do the Word (Matt. 7:24).
Take heed how you hear the Word (Luke 8:18).
Preach repentance and faith (Luke 24:47).
Learn from Him (Matt. 11:29).
Hear and see (Matt. 13:16).
Preach the Word (Mark 16:15).
Listen and respond (Mark 4:20).
Repent and believe (Mark 1:14).
Pray that God would send harvesters (Luke 10:2).
Abide in the Word (John 8:31).
If you don't believe Moses and the prophets you won't
   believe the resurrection (Luke 16:31).
Keep His commands (John 14:15).
Keep His Word (John 14:21).
Don't be fooled by false prophets (Luke 17:23).

A new adventure to enjoy

Be faithful in what you have been given (Luke 16:10).
Do good on the Sabbath (Luke 6:9).
Celebrate communion (Luke 22:19).
Let the children come (Mark 10:14–15).
Don't forbid miracle workers (Mark 9:38–39).
If you believe, all things are possible (Matt. 21:21).
Don't put old wine into new wineskins (Matt. 9:17).
Reach people – fish for men (John 21:6).

WHAT JESUS DIDN'T SAY

Many churches resemble academic institutions. This is not surprising given the word-based nature of faith, but is deeply hostile to people who are not remotely academic. Churches can give the impression that it is with much learning that we enter the kingdom of God. Jesus didn't say that Christianity is an academic pursuit for the learned but that it is for everyone whatever their academic level. It's all about a new kind of life, so don't be fooled when churches put on a learning-based curriculum and think that those who 'graduate' are now 'disciples'. Christ's coaching has a key thinking component, and learning and memorisation will be part of it, but He drives us to whole-life transformation, not just the brain, and it goes on for the rest of your life, not just a set number of weeks.

MAIN POINTS

- Christ coaches us by His teaching in the Bible and our reflection on that teaching as we live life with Him.
- There are many areas in which He will instruct us, if we let Him.
- His teaching is not given that we should just expand our knowledge but that we should live the new kind of life He promises.

ACTION

1. Next time you read a command of Jesus, talk to Him about it. Tell Him what you really feel. Do you warm to it? Find it too difficult? Allow Jesus to apply the command specifically.
2. Ask Jesus to illuminate areas where you may be struggling to obey. If appropriate, ask a trusted friend to help you identify areas. Sometimes we are too hard on ourselves, sometimes not nearly hard enough.

Chapter 4

If you can't trust Jesus, who can you trust?

Jack Grout would not be known outside his immediate circle of family, friends and the golf club where he worked, were it not for the man he coached. Jack Grout was the coach of Jack Nicklaus, the winner of 18 major golf tournaments and widely regarded as the finest golfer who ever played the game. He was the Tiger Woods of his day. Grout has since passed away but when Nicklaus was at the height of his fame he would still go to Jack Grout at the start of every golf season at Scioto Club in Columbus, Ohio, and ask Grout to teach him how to play golf. Grout would take Nicklaus through the fundamentals of grip, set up and swing path, as if he were playing the game for the first time.

Trust in such a relationship is crucial. You need to know that the advice received is going to help. Although it's not life and death (golfers just feel it is), minor adjustments to the golf swing can make a big difference, and only the best coaches can spot the problem.

If you are thinking of hiring a coach, you want to avoid coaches with quirky methods or odd personalities by talking to other clients about their approach. When you have a session you need to assess whether you like what they say. Can you trust them?

When it comes to the coaching of Jesus, our need for trust is no less great. A Christian will ideally assess His reliability before committing to learn from Him, but it's amazing how many don't.

Many respond to Christ without fully realising who He is and what this might mean. So if we are being coached by Christ we need to be as sure as we can be that we can trust Him, especially as some of His teaching may sound strange first time around.

Why can you trust Jesus?

1. This is God you are listening to

Deciding that Jesus was God in human flesh was not easy for the early followers. It represented a seismic shift in thinking for faithful Jews who knew their Old Testament and how separate God was from humankind. Yet at the same time He is the Creator who loves people and wants friendship with them, in spite of their reluctance to involve Him in their life. He had made friendship agreements (covenants) with the people of Israel and not given up on them when they let Him down. The laws in the Old Testament were their laws, the stories part of their heritage, the prophets had predicted a glorious future that they would enjoy. When Jesus came, they saw Him as a great teacher, maybe even the Messiah (the Anointed One) God had promised. But they saw the Messiah as a political figure, not a meek servant, so it took time for them to grasp that He was God, too. As Jews, the thought was too blasphemous to contemplate.

But Jesus was very aware who He was. In Mark we discover that early on, 'the Son of Man [ie Jesus] is Lord even of the Sabbath' (Mark 2:28). After the healing of the man lowered through the roof, Jesus says He has 'authority to forgive sins' (something only God did). In the temptation narrative where Jesus is confronted by Satan, He is asked in Matthew 4:6, if He is the Son of God, and Jesus never denies that He is. Later He explicitly says, 'I am the way and the truth and the life. No-one comes to the Father except through me' (John 14:6). There are many other clear occasions where the Gospel writers make it clear that the words of Jesus are one with the words of God His Father.

Our Coach's words are the truth, and won't be bettered by anyone else. They are the most important words we will ever hear. Nothing else we ever read will have such relevance for us. We give thanks for the human intelligence and wisdom that serves society in a whole range of fields, but make no mistake; Jesus' wisdom on life is the final word and cannot be bettered.

2. His teaching is gripping

Christians take it for granted that the teaching of Jesus is seen as the authoritative teaching of the Church, but when a Galilean peasant left His carpentry to commence His public ministry, few people knew who He was. It was left to John the Baptist to announce that the Messiah was coming, but even he had his doubts later on. There was no one managing a publicity campaign for Jesus. He was starting from scratch. His reputation, at least in the early days, depended entirely on what He said. If no one had listened, or chosen to seek Him out, there was no one asking that He be given a second chance. What we find is that people wanted to listen to Jesus. The common people heard Him gladly. They were astonished and amazed at His teaching, staggered that He spoke with such authority (Mark 1:27). In Luke 19:47 authorities tried to kill Him but couldn't because of His popularity. Even if we weren't wanting to be coached by Him, we would have to acknowledge with many scholars and critics down through the centuries that Jesus' teaching is worthy of study and consideration.

3. We have four witnesses

Although many have questioned whether the teaching of the Gospels really does reflect the teaching of Jesus, no one has come up with a convincing reason why four men would fabricate their accounts with an astonishing overlap of evidence. The four Gospels are a unique genre of literature that Bible scholars have struggled to define. They are like a biography, but miss out too much of Jesus' life to be classed 'biography'. They are written as history, but don't include sufficient detail to make them historical works. They include theological reflection but are certainly not a systematic explanation of doctrine. After considering all the different options, one scholar merely concluded, 'They are books about Jesus'!

Matthew and John were members of the Twelve. Mark was a convert who leaned heavily on the apostle Peter, and Luke was a Gentile doctor who worked closely with the apostle Paul. These were men who were compelled by the Holy Spirit to record the life of Christ, His teaching, miracles and key events of His life, most notably His death and resurrection. His life is not given as the sole observation of one person but the combined understanding of men whose own lives had been transformed by the new kind of life He brings.

4. It's teaching that is at one with the rest of the New Testament

Attempts have been made to set the teaching of Jesus against the other New Testament writers, as if they are at odds with each other. The rest of the New Testament helps us to understand the way in which the Early Church lived out Jesus' teaching. The book of Acts and the letters explain what living as a Christian meant for people who were located in various parts of the Roman world. We find the rest of the New Testament giving further clarity and understanding of the implications of the coming of Jesus. It unpacks the significance of the death and resurrection of Christ and reminds us how His coming slots into God's wider programme to one day reconcile to Himself all things in heaven and earth under Christ.

If the rest of the New Testament ignored the teaching of Jesus we would conclude that it was teaching for the early disciples with no abiding relevance. But we find that the New Testament writers are concerned that the communities which grow up are focused on following Christ and becoming like Him. The followers of Jesus became known as 'Christians' by the non-churchgoers – a nickname meaning literally 'little Christs' (Acts 11:26). In Paul's epistles we find a similar call to holy living that we find in the teaching of Jesus.

Compare, for example, Jesus' command in the Sermon on the Mount, 'Be perfect, therefore, as your heavenly Father is perfect' (Matt. 5:48), with other passages in the New Testament: 'Be imitators of God, therefore' (Eph. 5:1); 'just as he who called you is holy, so be holy in all you do' (1 Pet. 1:15); 'Whoever claims to live in him must walk as Jesus did' (1 John 2:6). The whole of the New Testament is encouraging us to live this new kind of life.

The major difference in writing after the Gospels is that the rest of the New Testament writers can stress the dynamic of the Holy Spirit as enabling, with our co-operation, the changes to take place.

This book focuses on the teaching of Jesus as recorded in the Gospels, but He continues to teach by His Spirit throughout the New Testament. When Luke opens the book of Acts, he tells Theophilus that his Gospel concerned what Jesus had 'begun' to do and teach. Luke was saying that Jesus was still alive, and still at work and here's what He's doing. The early chapters of Revelation include words from the lips of the risen Jesus for churches in Asia Minor. There are things we need to know that Jesus didn't cover in His three years of public ministry.

5. It's teaching for today

Some of Jesus' teaching and His approach was only relevant for the Twelve. Jesus directs them to go to 'the lost sheep of Israel' and gives specific direction on how they should go, what they should take and how they should depend on the villages they went to (Matt. 10). He trained 12 Jewish men, symbolising the new thing that God was doing in Israel, a people formed historically of 12 tribes.

But this was interim – Jesus was creating the basis of a new community, one that would soon expand to include all people groups, and include men and women. Even during His ministry, a Samaritan woman became an early evangelist (John 4) and Jesus uses women to spread the news of His resurrection.

If some of the teaching was for there and then, the vast majority is for here and now. The Gospels were written (probably between AD 55 and 90) by men inspired to record the life and message of Jesus so that the Church could follow what He said. We noted in Chapter 1 that at the end of his Gospel, Matthew records what the Church calls the Great Commission, where Jesus tells His disciples to 'Go and make disciples of all nations'. What is often missed is the way they are to do this. Disciples are made by teaching them to 'do' everything He has commanded them to do. As far as the Gospel writers were concerned, the followers of Jesus were to be defined by what they did in response to His Word. Similarly, John says at the end of his Gospel that 'these [things] are written that you may believe that Jesus is the Christ' (John 20:31). Belief means 'put your confidence in' – John has selected the sayings and events of Jesus' life so we would know where to put our confidence, and know that the Coach is reliable. Today, disciples are male and female, Jew and Gentile, and we interpret and apply the Gospels as those who have received the promised Spirit. The teaching of the new life comes to you and me as if from the lips of Jesus.

What Jesus didn't say

Jesus never said that we couldn't trust Him with everything, as if there might be areas where He was deficient. Some Christians lock Jesus into a first-century AD time bubble and assume that He has no knowledge of life in the twenty-first, as if He would be hopeless at the keyboard of a PC and ignorant of the workings of the Internet. There's no subject that He couldn't speak on with clarity and insight. If you pray to Him about finding a solution to a problem, you needn't give Him a rudimentary lesson to explain what you are on about. He knows. He's clever. He can help. He's just waiting to be asked.

Main points

- We need to be sure that our Coach can be trusted.
- The Gospels underline that Jesus is God. We can be sure that the words we read are His words and will meet our needs and circumstances.
- Jesus' teaching is one with the rest of the New Testament, which also confirms the centrality of entering into and enjoying a new kind of life.

Action

1. Consider the words that influence you each day. How do the words of Jesus rate?
2. Think about the teaching of Jesus that you find most difficult to understand, and determine to find out what He is really saying. Talk to a Christian leader about how it should be interpreted.
3. Are there areas that you struggle with that you haven't spoken to Him about?

Chapter 5

Jesus is a super-model

Advertisers say that product association happens at a subliminal level. Few people actually think, 'If I had those football boots I would play like Zinedine Zidane' (the France and Real Madrid player), but the fact that he plays in Adidas boots means that, faced with the choice, people will choose Adidas over another product if they admire his play. So if you are an advertiser, pick someone whom people admire, pay them big bucks to use the product, get them on film, hope they don't do something stupid in the meantime and you will outsell your competitors. Advertisers are tapping into the most natural of human instincts – the need to imitate others. Aren't you glad you picked up the rudiments of table-manners, dressing and toilet training before you left home? But it's not just children that imitate. We all do. We observe behaviour we like and think, 'Mmm, I must try that,' and we observe behaviour we believe stinks and think, 'You wouldn't catch me doing that'. Karaoke singing? Bungee jumping? Train spotting? No thanks. And the weird thing is that we are not always aware of why we don't fancy a particular activity. It just isn't us.

Many people look at the life of Jesus and find that, quite frankly, they don't want to be like Him. And the sad thing is that many of these people are Christians. They know they should be excited about Christian growth, but when it comes to it they run a mile from the sort of Jesus they think they are being pushed towards. They believe the morals of Christ, but don't like the model of Christ they have been given.

If there are doubts in your mind about whether you want to be like Jesus, then the whole process of 'coaching' to be like Him is likely to stall. Here's why. What is heroic for us becomes embedded within us. We find we have a secret hankering to be like people that, in our more sober moments, we know shouldn't be attractive; a love 'em and leave 'em Casanove, or a wily business executive who gets even on her enemies. Our imaginations are not automatically transformed when we come to Christ, yet it is out of the heart's longings that we live. Our personality and aspirations have developed over time and are not easily displaced by a quick burst of the relevant verses. We like our quirky behaviour, after all, it is part of us. It was a shock to my teenage system to realise that the cool hard man persona of 'Clint Eastwood characters in spaghetti Westerns' had become heroic to me in a way that Jesus wasn't. How driven are you by your heroes?

The solution comes as we undergo a change in our thinking, feeling and choosing areas, which we will look at in Part Three. But we also need to ensure that we have the Jesus of the Gospels firmly in our heads, and not the Jesus of the imagination of the modern Church and modern culture. American journalist and bestselling author, Philip Yancey, wrote the book, *The Jesus I Never Knew*, because he discovered that the Jesus of his youth was nothing like the real thing. Jesus was a super-model and he didn't realise it.

The real Jesus

If you had spent time with Jesus when He was on earth what would you have found? You would have found a man who seemed normal at one level – He ate, drank, laughed, wept, slept and talked just as we do. He was great to have around, fun at parties but equally comfortable having a chat over a drink. He would be top of your list of invites for any gathering. There was nothing obviously unworldly about Him. He was so normal that it took a while for the disciples to accept that it was God Himself who had spent three years with them.

Jesus lived in the kingdom of God (where what God wants done is done) all the time; there was nothing Jesus said or did which was out of step with His Father. He expresses the character of God perfectly, mingling justice, mercy, love, compassion, joy and peace in a way that made Him a joy to know. When He saw something out of sync with God's purposes He did something about it. As He travelled around the Galilee region His touch meant the blind were able to see, the lame could walk, the demonised were freed from bondage. On one occasion 5,000-plus were able to gorge themselves on the product of five loaves and two fish. He changed the weather so the lake of Galilee became calm. There were even occasions of the dead being raised.

His extraordinary handling of people is a compelling feature of His life – a woman caught in adultery is saved, literally, from a mob baying for blood. The mob receive a lesson in judging others and she is told to leave her life of sin (see John 8:1–11). Then there is a religious leader, expecting an argument, or at the very least an explanation, but receives instead a rebuke for not grasping the basics of Old Testament readings pointing to the need for a spiritual new birth (see John 3:1–21). And amid all this He comes across as incredibly relaxed, trusting His Father with His life; on one occasion a great storm is raging and He's fast asleep. How cool is that?

Jesus' encounters led to change and His teaching led to change. People forgave those who had messed them about, blessed those that cursed them, trusted God rather than worried, spoke honestly when manipulation might be easier. Jesus was demonstrating in His life that God was starting a new era in human affairs. From now on people's relationship with God would depend on their relationship with Him. This was the Anointed One that the Old Testament pointed to. He was showing the world a new way of living, in relationship with God, a return to the way things had been when Adam and Eve had first enjoyed paradise with God. When Jesus tells His disciples to teach people to obey His commands, He is asking that His manner of life be replicated in those that followed Him. His closest friend, the apostle John, would later write, 'Whoever claims to live in him must walk as Jesus did' (1 John 2:6).

A Jesus-shaped you

In life we come across people who bring out the best in us: allow us to be ourselves yet also draw us on to become something better. When we are with them, doing the right thing seems easy. Jesus is like that. Adulations such as 'great guy', 'terrific sport', 'a real diamond,' 'gold dust', could have been coined with Him in mind. He is truly heroic and if we were thinking clearly, we would want to be like Him, always.

So part of our re-education into the new kind of life is to acknowledge that the Jesus of the Bible is the sort of person we should want to become, even if we know deep down that we don't want to. Acknowledgement of our private fears about the sort of person God might make us is a key step to change. This may not happen overnight. Later we look at some of the ways Jesus uses to coach us to truly want the changes that He has in mind; for now we may take comfort from knowing that our essential personality is unlikely to be radically altered. Jesus doesn't want clones, but our character is to be like His. There's a Jesus compassion, a Jesus joy, a Jesus hope, a Jesus peace, to isolate just a few attributes. It's a change in the inner life that will pop out with your DNA on it. These changes come as we co-operate with Him, and truly want them. Contrary to some wild claims, God doesn't impose anything on us, though He does urge us to change.

WHAT JESUS DIDN'T SAY

The path to Christ-likeness is paved with pleasant-sounding words, but rarely with good intentions. Deep down most Christians have a picture of Jesus that is out of their range and so they content themselves with tinkering at the parts of their life that they can handle. Un-Christlike behaviour is assumed to be normal, and expected in many Christian communities.

A rigid application of doing what Jesus does, does not mean we become like Jesus was, just as singing the right words in the right order, doesn't make us sound as good as Pavarotti. 'Being' comes before 'doing' as we will see in the rest of this book.

Main points:
- Many people don't want to be like the Jesus they imagine.
- We need to recognise our reluctance to imitate the kind of Jesus we think about or we will never make progress.
- Jesus is the sort of person everyone would want to be like if they were thinking clearly.

Action
1. Consider the aspects of Jesus' character you like most and those you like least. Talk to God about them.
2. Spend some time reading about Jesus in the Gospels and ask God to give you a heart to be like Him. Unless you get to the point where you want to be like Christ, you won't be. Chapters 12 to 16 will be key ones for your thinking.

PART TWO

Grasp the Fundamentals

Progress towards becoming like Jesus with the new kind of life that He promises, means being clear about the way in which we need to change.

This section looks at some fundamental teaching that we need to grasp if we want to see change.

We must start with acknowledging our fundamental problem of our rebellion against God – what the Bible calls sin.

This inner rebellion requires God's intervention if we are to be alive spiritually, and His continuing work if we are to embrace the new kind of life and deal with the old.

We look next in more detail at the Holy Spirit's work of bringing us to new life, and the necessity of His ongoing involvement in every act we make towards our increasing growth.

We need to understand how Christ's teaching functions in our lives or we will find that His words are as disabling to us as the Old Testament law became to some Jews.

Progress is not always as smooth as we would like, so we look at the ways in which our Coach has anticipated this in His teaching.

Prayer is a vital part of our development. We invite Him to be at work, we share with Him our needs and grow to know and understand His ways.

Chapter 6

Change comes from the inside

In his book *Transforming Grace*, Jerry Bridges talks about the two ways in which US companies can file for bankruptcy. Directors can file for temporary bankruptcy or final bankruptcy: temporary bankruptcy provides a hedge from creditors so they can get back on their feet, total bankruptcy comes when they reach the end of their resources. They know the company is over and there's no way back, they lock the office doors and don't come back.[1]

Many people realise they have done wrong before God and so file for temporary bankruptcy hoping to clean up their act so God will be pleased with them. But Jesus is very clear about this approach – we cannot do it. His harshest criticism was for the self-righteous and religious in His day, the Pharisees and teachers of the law who claimed that their ability to (so they thought) keep the commands of God fitted them for the kingdom. They thought they were OK because they performed the correct religious acts, and stayed out of jail. Jesus didn't mince His words in His description of them: 'You snakes! You brood of vipers! How will you escape being condemned to hell?' (Matt. 23:33).

There was so much confusion about what did and didn't please God that Jesus had to continually clarify what sin was, especially with His own followers: 'What comes out of a man is what makes him "unclean". For from within, out of men's hearts, come evil thoughts, sexual immorality, theft, murder, adultery, greed, malice, deceit, lewdness, envy, slander, arrogance and folly. All these evils come from inside and make a man "unclean"' (Mark 7:20–23).

We fail to realise we need the grace of God. You can do whatever you like to appear clean, but the bad smell is still there, and it comes from within you.

We need to accept the bad news, that we need coaching more badly than we think we do. But once we realise we are totally bankrupt, things can look up as we grasp the benefits of Christ's life, death and resurrection, and then allow Him to change us so that we become the sort of person that changes from the inside out.

The foundation – Christ's death and resurrection

We can admit our total bankruptcy because of the total sufficiency of what Jesus offers in the new kind of life. This new life is based on what Jesus did in His life, death and resurrection. The New Testament writers use a number of pictures to describe how we should understand what happened when Jesus died. Mark quotes Jesus as saying He had come to give His 'life as a ransom for many' (Mark 10:45). His death was a deliberate act on His part; arranged by the Jewish leaders, in conjunction with their Roman occupiers, yet Jesus gave up His life voluntarily.

He times His death to show that what God had done in the Old Testament, He was doing again. His death coincided with the Passover celebration, when the Jews commemorated what God did through Moses in the first exodus when the Jews were enslaved in Egypt 1,300 years before. When evil was at its worst, God acted to judge Egypt and save Israel. When the angel of death saw the blood of a lamb put on the doorframes by the Israelites, he passed over the homes. Now Jesus would become the Passover lamb, in a deliberate act of self-sacrifice. His blood would be sufficient to avert God's anger against the sin of all who would trust in Him, and His glorious resurrection would be proof that God had accepted His Son's death.

So when you and I put our confidence in Jesus, God makes sure that His death on the cross counts for us. When His blood is 'applied to our life' the angel of death passes over us. Our sins, past, present and future, including the sort of stuff in Mark 7:20–23 above, are included – nothing is left out. We are in a new standing with God. In John 1:12 we read: 'Yet to all who received him, to those who believed in his name, he gave the right to become children of God ...'. John 3:16 famously says, 'For God so loved the world that he gave his one and only Son, that whoever believes in him should not perish but have eternal life.'

People were to come to Him to enjoy His life and reject other ways of living. Jesus put it like this: 'And anyone who does not carry his cross and follow me cannot be my disciple' (Luke 14:27). It's a little like saying that unless I abandon my plans to fly to Sydney, Australia, I can't go to New York. It is not that the New York airport authorities won't let me in, just that I can't do one unless I do the other. We can't follow Jesus if we prefer a lifestyle that is opposed to Him – it is an impossibility.

New life

So how does our Coach work to enable change?
Here are some views:

- All we need to do is to ask for forgiveness and we will be saved for eternity.
- We need to prove that we have truly repented, by living for Christ.
- God does His bit in saving us, now we do our bit in becoming like Jesus.

Which is correct?

To answer, we need to clarify those parts of our growth where we are active in the process and those parts where we are passive.

The events of Christ's life, death and resurrection occurred in human history. We were totally passive. Christians who say they need to do nothing to contribute to their salvation are in that sense correct – God's salvation plan is watertight. But having been rescued it is our work to co-operate with God in cleaning ourselves up. We can't do it without Him, but equally, He won't do it without us!

I have been fortunate with sporting injuries. My only major problem was a damaged ankle playing football for London Bible College (now London School of Theology). I limped off unaware of the damage and it was only when a friend suggested that maybe I needed a trip to A & E that I realised what had happened. The x-ray showed a fractured fibula needing manipulation by a surgeon under general anaesthetic. Once the surgeon had done his work a cast could be made and the bone could start to knit back together. The biggest shock was two months later seeing the emaciated muscle on my right leg which needed building if I was to be back playing before the season ended. Walking, then light weights, then running, and the strength started to return and the muscles soon matched my left leg.

I needed the intervention of an outside force, but then I needed to exercise the muscle. The new kind of life needs to be lived with your conscious co-operation. You need to intend to grow, to want to grow. As you co-operate with your Coach, you can be sure that He is right there with you.

In this book we will see how the Holy Spirit enables all the changes God has planned for you. We will see how you co-operate with the changes in thinking, feeling and choosing so that you start to change from the inside out.

But to return to the earlier views. Is it just about 'trusting God'? Imagine if I had asked my wife when we were engaged what was the minimum love I needed to show in order to act properly as a husband? How would she have felt? Asking the question pours doubt on my commitment.

God loves us unconditionally and grace is showered upon us; nothing we can do would or could repay God, and no response from us could be 'acceptable'. But a true response to this grace as children of God, is to want to be like our Father, showing the family likeness and knowing the new kind of life where we progressively change from the inside out. Christ calls for us to abandon ourselves and know new life in Him – that's what repentance is. There is no 'minimum requirement' – it's all God's grace, but if you are asking the question, maybe you haven't understood what God's grace for you is really like?

The pastor of an evangelical church went on retreat to a Franciscan monastery. He was anxious about what might happen, this being his first time at a retreat. But he came away impressed by the words of his 'spiritual director' for the retreat: 'The only thing you truly own is your sin, everything else is a gift.' Jesus wants to teach you and me how to daily deny ourselves and follow Him, giving us such a thrilling view of walking with God that we are too excited by His gift to want to live with the 'sin' to which we are so attached.

What Jesus didn't say

Jesus didn't say that if you merely pray a prayer asking for forgiveness from God that all will be well. He didn't say that if you put your hand up at an evangelistic meeting, all would be well. These may be the means whereby you respond to Christ's free gift of salvation, but the salvation He offers involves us repenting from sin and continuing to follow Christ on a daily basis as He helps us; not a one-off decision which we subsequently ignore. Of course we are not strong enough ourselves to 'keep going' and that's why God provides all we need to continue, through Christ's coaching and the work of His Spirit.

Main points

- We are totally bankrupt.
- Jesus' death and resurrection brings forgiveness for all who put their confidence in Him.
- We need to work with Christ so that the victory over sin at the cross is reproduced in our lives.
- If we understand God's grace we will want to give ourselves fully in service of Him.

Action

1. Are you trying to live the Christian life without realising you can't?
2. Think about ways in which you regularly struggle. What would you like God to do for you?
3. Church tends to grade sin into the acceptable and unacceptable. Determine that you will judge yourself by the Word of God,

not other people, and ask God to help you maintain a humble attitude when you see others behaving in ways you used to.

4. Are there sins that are so much a part of you that you wouldn't know what to do without them?

Note

1. Jerry Bridges, *Transforming Grace* (Navpress, 1991).

Chapter 7

With God involved, failure is not an option

The comparison of sporting heroes across the generations makes for good pub conversation and phone-ins on radio shows. Who is the greatest footballer ever? Was it the Brazilian Pelé, the Dutchman Johann Cruyff, the Argentinian Diego Maradona or Frenchman Zinedene Zidane?

In cricket who was the best all-rounder – Ian Botham of England or West Indian Gary Sobers? In sprinting would Marion Jones have been beaten Florence Griffith-Joyner? In cycling would Miguel Indurain beat Lance Armstrong if both were at their peak performance? What would be the outcome of a tennis match between Martina Navratilova and Billy Jean King? Of course the debates are essentially about opinion. We will never know. All you can truly say is that they each have been widely regarded as the best when they played.

When we compare ourselves with Christians in the past, we imagine that the Jesus class of AD 33 would pulverise all comers in any imaginary battle in the closeness to God stakes. They had after all a major advantage over all who walk in their footsteps – one-to-one encounters with Jesus. They had the skills of the finest of all coaches to help them; infallible insights, perfect love, expert direction. Since our theme is 'coached by Jesus' you would expect me to champion the parallels between the Twelve and us today. In fact I believe the reverse – we are in a *better* position than the Twelve. I say this because the Holy Spirit has been given to all who choose to follow (and therefore be coached by) Christ. He brings the new kind of life to us in a way that the disciples would only come to fully know when they received Him for themselves.

John the Baptist said that Jesus would baptise (immerse) His followers in the Holy Spirit, just as he, John, had in water (John 1:32–33), but this didn't take place in Jesus' earthly life. In John 14 Jesus refers to the Spirit who would come later as One, just like Him, who would be with them when He had gone. Jesus' presence with them was limited to the times when He was around; when the Spirit came He would be with them forever – which means that you and I can know the presence of the living Christ all the time, wherever we are.

Jesus' instructions for making new disciples included baptising them in the name of the Father, Son and Holy Spirit; ie involvement with and experience of the triune God: Father, Son and Holy Spirit. The Holy Spirit relates to our spirit in such a way that it's like having Jesus (or indeed God) with us. The coming of the Spirit is fulfilled in Acts 2 after Jesus had died, risen and ascended back to His Father.

TIME LINE

Old Testament	
Genesis 1–2	Holy Spirit involved
Old Testament history Exodus to Esther	Holy Spirit at work in individuals at specific times, eg Samson, Saul, David, Elijah, Elisha, the prophets
Old Testament prophecy Isaiah to Malachi	Holy Spirit directs prophets to speak the Word for then, and the future.
New Testament	
Pre-Jesus' ministry	Holy Spirit promised by John the Baptist
Jesus' ministry	Holy Spirit anoints and equips Jesus
Breath of Spirit (John 20:22)	Disciples receive anticipatory filling

Jesus' teaching With Nicodemus (John 3:1–21) To the crowds (John 7) With the Twelve (John 14–17)	Holy Spirit anticipated by Jesus
Acts 2	Believers receive Holy Spirit on the Day of Pentecost
Acts 8:17; 10:47; 19:6	eg of Samaritans; Gentiles; disciples of John – receiving/ being baptised in the Spirit
Romans 12; 1 Corinthians 12; Ephesians 4	Spiritual gifts described
Galatians 5	Spiritual fruit described

Who is He?

Jesus describes the Spirit as the 'paraclete', which can be translated in various ways: Strengthener, Counsellor, Helper, Supporter, Advisor, Ally, Senior Friend.

These words help to de-mystify the Spirit whose work has been largely misunderstood within many parts of the Church. When we come to God the Father we may conjure up thoughts of One who works as a good earthly Father might. We have the portrait of Jesus as a Person in the Gospels. But the words 'Holy Spirit' don't sound personal and some imagine Him as a fluid that fills us or as an emotion that overcomes us. If we take our cues from Jesus, we will be OK. He has exactly the same character qualities as Jesus.

What He does

1. He convicts of sin

When Jesus spoke of the coming of the Spirit in His long seminar with the Twelve in the Upper Room just prior to His death, He said that it was good that He was leaving them because then He could ask the Father to send them the Holy Spirit (John 16:7). The Spirit would have a convicting role, working in people's hearts as a prosecutor so that they might realise where life is to be found and why Jesus had come. So, when you became aware of your sinfulness, it was because the Spirit alerted you to the truth about God, and He still performs this role as we sin. A growing follower gets to recognise His work within.

2. He gives life

We saw in the last chapter that the new kind of life comes when we are born again (literally 'born from above'). Jesus told Nicodemus, 'no-one can see the kingdom of God unless he is born again' (John 3:3). The active Person in this process is the Holy Spirit, who is at work within us enabling us to respond to the gospel and imparting the new kind of life to us.

3. He makes Christ real to us

Jesus tells His followers that when the Spirit comes to them, 'He will bring glory to me by taking from what is mine and making it known to you' (John 16:14).

So what is made known to us? Commenting on this verse, J.I. Packer says:

> He must have meant, at least everything that is real and true about me as God incarnate, as the Father's agent in creation, providence and grace, as this world's rightful lord, and as the one who is actually master of it whether men acknowledge it or not. But surely he also meant, all that is true about me as your divine lover, your mediator, your surety in the new covenant, your prophet, priest and king ... all this is true of me as your shepherd, husband and friend, your life and your hope, the author and finisher of your faith, the lord of your own personal history, and the one who will one day bring you to be with me and share my glory, who am thus your path and prize.[1]

It is an extraordinary promise – the Spirit's ministry to us, means our Coach, though external to us and at the right hand of the Father, is also within us, making His presence known and felt.

4. He empowers us for service

It was the presence of the Spirit that transformed the nervous and hesitant followers in Jerusalem, huddled together afraid that they would be killed like Jesus, into spiritual warriors taking the truth of Christ to the people of Jerusalem and on into the rest of the Roman world.

The Spirit's coming was always plan A in their coaching programme and remains today vital for anyone wanting to make progress. He has already been at work in your life far more than you realise and will work with you as much as you allow Him. Remember the illustration of the house in Chapter 2. There is no limit to how much you can know God. There are no restrictions apart from the ones you place there yourself.

This is reinforced by pretty well every page of the New Testament; the apostles reinforce the ethical teaching of Jesus, urging new believers to chuck out sinful habits and welcome the Spirit's ministry.

5. He enables us to change

We won't behave like Jesus did until we become like Jesus was. The Holy Spirit who lives within us can so transform our interior – the way we think and feel and choose – that we become like Jesus (see Part Three).

Jesus hints at this when He gives the disciples the picture of a vine in John 15 and compares them to the branches. A branch wrenched away from the vine has no life within it. You and I have the potential to change because we are part of Christ, indwelt by His Spirit, but we need to remain in the vine. In context, this means us submitting to the Word of Christ, and intending to develop as He directs us. We can quench and grieve the Spirit. He is a Person who is offended when we sin. Many Christians know little of His empowering because they fail to give Him prominence. The great news is that, as we intend to grow, God draws alongside us to make it possible. We will need to learn how, by understanding God and ourselves better. But there is no limit to how much we can know God in our lives, other than limits we place ourselves. With God involved, failure is not an option.

WHAT JESUS DOESN'T SAY

That the presence of the Spirit may provoke an emotional reaction is clear, just as we 'feel something' when we meet a friend. If we have squeezed Him out of our lives we might find welcoming Him back a memorable time. But that is not to equate Him with emotion. We feel emotional for all sorts of reasons and many will have little to do with Him. All of which links with the common error of waiting until we feel 'His presence' before acting for God, as if we need to be overcome before we can act effectively. Jesus commands us to obey Him, deal with sin and share His good news. Whether we feel confident and excited, or dull and apathetic, is irrelevant to our need to respond to the coaching of Christ. We can be sure that the Spirit is with us at all times and whenever we serve Him and need His help, He will be there.

MAIN POINTS

- We know Christ through the Holy Spirit and so have His constant presence, unlike the Twelve during Jesus' time on earth.
- The Spirit is at work to convict, make Christ known to us, empower and enable us to change. If we co-operate with His changes to the inside, the outside will follow.
- The Holy Spirit's work is to help us do what we couldn't naturally do – become like Jesus from the inside.

ACTION

1. Acknowledge and welcome the presence of the Holy Spirit.
2. Co-operate as God transforms you from being focused on self, driven by instinct and self-interest following your own inclinations, to focusing on God and living as He has commanded.
3. Determine to let Him teach you through your study of the Scriptures and through those gifted at explaining the Bible.
4. Ask Christ to coach you so that you are able to recognise His inner promptings. Act on what He says and reflect on the experience.

Note

1. J.I. Packer, *Keep in Step With the Spirit* (IVP, 1984).

Chapter 8

It is not good news if you don't lay down the law

Mike was wondering what had hit him. He was a sensitive guy who had become a Christian at a school CU weekend away on the Isle of Wight. Friends had urged him to read the Gospels for himself if he wanted his faith to develop. So he did. He began with Matthew chapter 1 and although he struggled to see the relevance of the list of names at the start of the chapter he settled down when he read the Christmas narrative. He was OK until he hit chapter 5: the Sermon on the Mount.

He read: 'You have heard that it was said to the people long ago, "Do not murder, and anyone who murders will be subject to judgment." But I tell you that anyone who is angry with his brother will be subject to judgment' (Matt. 5:21–22).

Mike guessed that 'brother' meant wider than blood relative, but it so happened that his brother James had lost his favourite CD and Mike was livid.

Later on he read: 'You have heard that it was said, "Do not commit adultery." But I tell you that anyone who looks at a woman lustfully has already committed adultery with her in his heart' (Matt. 5:27–28).

Mike's mind went to Jo in the sixth form, in fact he had been able to think of little else since she had joined the school a month before.

He wasn't doing too well. He had also puzzled over, '... unless your righteousness surpasses that of the Pharisees and the teachers of the law, you will certainly not enter the kingdom of heaven' (Matt. 5:20). Weren't the scribes and Pharisees regarded as the most godly and pious in the whole of Israel? And to cap it all, Jesus even says, 'Be perfect, therefore, as your heavenly Father is perfect' (Matt. 5:48).

By now Mike was a mess. He was OK with the idea of cleaning up his act, but Jesus was saying that the motivations that lead to those actions were wrong too. He had heard that Jesus had fulfilled the law for us, paid the price that we couldn't pay – so why did he now find that Jesus' commands seem to take things up a notch? He had signed up to a new kind of life, so he thought. But there seemed to be several counties between his life and what Jesus was calling him to.

Mike didn't know that he wasn't the first to fall at the first fence. Such demands cause some to discount the teaching of Jesus, and the Sermon on the Mount in particular, as not to be followed literally. 'Expect to fail,' they say, 'and don't worry about it.' The argument sounds OK until we realise that Jesus wasn't teaching for fun. He intended His followers to do the business. Jesus didn't say to His disciples: 'Look, you are going to fail, so don't worry about following Me. Just go back home until three years time, when I will have died and risen, then trust in Me so that your sins can be forgiven and you'll be OK for heaven.' He said no such thing. He called them to follow Him, to live like He did in the kingdom of God. They were far from perfect, frequently made mistakes, often got the wrong end of the stick, but they kept following.

Mike wisely went to see his pastor who, fortunately for him, understood how we should take the commands of the Law and of Jesus. This is what he was told.

1. The commands stand
Jesus never denied the validity of the Old Testament Law. God didn't have second thoughts about what was good and what was bad between the Old and New Testaments. If you want to 'be good' you obey the Law. But the Old Testament is like a sentence that is left half finished. It partly makes sense but it needed completing with

the coming of Jesus. Indeed you will make a whole host of errors if you don't see the Bible as a whole. The ditty, 'the new is in the old revealed, the old is in the new revealed', sums things up well.

2. We follow Jesus, the law keeper

But most importantly, Jesus tells us that He has fulfilled the Law (Matt. 5:17). Fulfilling the Law meant that Jesus is the righteousness to which the Law points; He is the permanent answer to the problem of human sin and unrighteousness for which the sacrificial system had provided a stop gap. Scripture teaches that these sacrifices pointed ahead to Jesus' perfect and final sacrifice on the cross so we wouldn't need to keep the law. Jesus is the restoration of Israel for which the prophets hoped – He does what Israel could not do, lived perfectly before God and keeps the covenant demands that Israel had failed to keep.

3. Jesus describes the new kind of life

All the way through the Sermon on the Mount Jesus is describing the new kind of life that is possible through relationship with Him. Mike is right to be dismayed because it is an impossible life. Outside of the working of the grace of God in our lives it is a recipe for extreme frustration. Some of the Jews had reckoned that they could keep the Law and God would be giving them high fives in celebration.

Jesus says it is what is inside that counts. He is looking for a higher standard than merely observing the letter of the Law – a heart standard that comes from the inner transformation of the Spirit of God. He does two things: He kept the Law fully so the righteous requirements are met in Him and our confidence in Him means we get the benefits. Secondly, He also sends His Spirit so that we can progressively live this new kind of life – the life that He would lead if He were us (as we saw in the last chapter). Jesus makes entrance into the kingdom dependent on a person's loyalty to Him and not on following the Law.

So Jesus represents the beginning of a new era: 'The Law and the Prophets were proclaimed until John. Since that time, the good news of the kingdom of God is being preached, and everyone is forcing his way into it' (Luke 16:16; Matt. 11:11–12).

Jesus preached 'gospel' not Law. Mike has to see the Sermon on the Mount as part of the gospel, not Law. Jesus' teaching does not function as something we must keep to please God but presumes the acceptance we know in Jesus' Person and ministry. If you treat the commands of Jesus as if they are laws, you will become even more screwed up than many of the Jews. It is not good news if you don't lay down the 'law'.

It is as if your fitness coach looks at you and says, 'You are a marathon runner. I am going to give you the training so that your status as marathon runner will be matched by your performance. Your training and nutrition will be of such a level that you will run the marathon easily. It will be as natural and effortless as walking to the shops.'

So we don't need to dodge the high ideals of Jesus. We can take Him at His word knowing that total failure is not an option. In Part Three we will see how we can co-operate with Christ to see the transformation of the whole person so that, bit by bit, we find that the impossible list of requirements, are doable – yes, even when your brother loses your CD and a fanciable girl joins the sixth form.

WHAT JESUS DIDN'T SAY

One of the reasons that professing Christians don't think they need coaching is that they abandon any sense that God expects them to obey the teaching of Jesus. They are so aware of God's free pardon through faith in Jesus' grace that they have little or no sense of shame for sin committed or failure to live as Jesus did. As Dallas Willard puts it: 'We're not only saved by grace, we're paralysed by it.'[1] We are brought into relationship with Jesus in spite of our inability to live as He taught. The disciples provide graphic examples of followers who are failures. But God's grace is not a one-off burst that is imparted at conversion to last until heaven. Jesus calls us to keep on following Him. We may struggle many times with the same habits; we may fail so much that we are embarrassed to call ourselves Christian. God understands and welcomes us back as we confess our sins and know Christ's daily help.

Main points

- Jesus' teaching seems even harder than the Old Testament Law.
- Jesus kept the Law perfectly.
- We have confidence that He has dealt with our sin, and joyfully learn from Him how to live.

Action

1. Thank God for the Law. It is wonderful that we know what pleases Him and it is a necessary yardstick to point us to Jesus.
2. Abandon your attempts to 'do your best' to please God. You can't. All you can do is receive Jesus' call to follow as a gift.
3. Look forward to discovering how Jesus wants you to change from the inside out, in the next chapters. Thank Him for setting before you a new kind of life and providing all you need to enjoy it.

Note

1. Unpublished article on Dallas Willard's website: 'Spiritual Formation: What it is, and How it is done'.

Chapter 9

We don't always make progress

When John came to see me I had a feeling that it wouldn't be a one-off visit. I was an assistant minister in Bournemouth and John had been attending our church for some weeks. He had been a Christian for six years, but despite a loving church fellowship in another part of Bournemouth, and what seemed from his description, to be wise counsel from his pastor, most of his Christian life had been going backwards. He had spent time in prison, gone back into taking drugs and been in trouble with the police. His old pastor believed he was throwing his salvation away.

I was able to assure him that Christ doesn't give up on people and wasn't about to start with him, but such stories raise an interesting dilemma: why do so many make such little progress? Why do we sometimes find that having been going well, we suddenly struggle, lose interest in God and even feel tempted to disappear back into a lifestyle we had said we shunned?

Jesus knew that we would be tripped up and so includes guidance in His teaching so that when a hiccough, or something serious, comes we can know what it is and talk it through with Him.

He lists six common errors that we do well to avoid:

1. Allowing Satan to divert us
2. Pursuing alternative attractions
3. Not being ready for the inevitable suffering

4. Remaining ignorant about God
5. Being disobedient
6. Remaining in unbelief
7. Mixing with the wrong Christians

1. Allowing Satan to divert us

In the parable of the sower recorded in Matthew 13, Jesus describes four types of soils that correspond to what happens to people who receive the Word of God. The first soil represents those who hear the Word of God but Satan snatches it away. D.A. Carson says: 'Some people hear the message about the kingdom; but like hardened paths, they do not let the truth penetrate, and before they really understand it the devil has snatched it away.'[1]

There is an unseen angelic being who opposes God and His work, and can influence us when we hear the Word of God, if we let him. Our Coach tells us to be careful to give attention to what we hear, lest we overlook it. Receiving the Word of God should be as vital as daily food. Jesus says to His disciples on one occasion, that He has food they knew nothing about, 'My food … is to do the will of him who sent me …' (John 4:32,34). In some cases we don't even allow the Word of God to be heard, our Bible gathers dust and we miss gathering with other believers. It's a prime reason we don't grow.

2. Pursuing alternative attractions

A singing coach might say to a pupil, 'You can't sing the top note unless you practise your scales.' She is not saying, 'I won't let you', rather that it is not going to happen. Jesus also says we aren't focused on the life-giving Word of God because we put our confidence in the wrong place, expecting life's wealth to produce the goods instead of God. This was the message of the second type of soil in the parable of the sower; for a time we find the alternative attractions sustain us. My friend John felt good when he took drugs and pursued the adventure of sailing close to the legal wind, you will have your own attractions that call to you at weak moments. Remember, the attractions are short-lived – don't be fooled by how pleasant they seem – they are like grenades with the pin out.

WE DON'T ALWAYS MAKE PROGRESS

3. Not being ready for suffering

Many start following Christ but give up when it becomes tough. In John's Gospel a large group stopped following Jesus when He told them about the cost (John 6:66). It hurts to tear ourselves away from our old habits and face a world that rejects Christ, but the new kind of life is worth following and of course there is a cost in not following, too. The joy of being in the kingdom makes any sacrifice worthwhile so anyone who ducks out for this reason is being foolish in the extreme, passing up the joy of knowing God both now and in eternity for apparent joy in the short term. The good news is that Jesus tells us we are blessed if we suffer for following Him. Our faith strengthens as God draws near to His child who is going through pain and we are reassured that it is worth it. But it does raise the question – are you prepared for the struggle that growth will sometimes bring?

4. Remaining ignorant about God

We will see later that thinking is a crucial part of our growth (Chapter 12). But thinking God's thoughts is only possible if we know what His thoughts are. The new kind of life is given birth and nurtured by the Word. Failure to know what God says or wants will mean we won't have a clue how to live. We may say we are Christ-followers but in practice follow at such a distance that we can't hear His voice at all.

So there is a whole wealth of biblical material which will help your growth that we can't begin to cover in a book this size. Jesus was speaking to people who knew who God was, and had some understanding of His dealings with His people in the past. This provides the framework of thinking about God. It is a treasure trove to be mined for the rest of our lives. God is good, He is love, He deals in justice with people. He always does what is for His glory and our ultimate good. His purposes for us are good and loving. If we could grasp them they would truly blow our mind. Eternity won't be long enough (as it were!) to discover how magnificent He is. God is gracious and leads us on from where we are to where He wants us to be, so if you think you know very little don't panic. But do use every means – sermons, small groups, tapes, videos, Internet to get to know as much as you can.

5. Being disobedient

We are also hampered in our growth when we know what we ought to do, but don't do it. Jesus tells a parable about two sons who are told to work. One says he will but doesn't, one says he won't but does. It is the doer who is commended. At the conclusion of the Sermon on the Mount we are told that anyone who does the Word is like a man who builds his house on a rock (Matt. 7:24). The one who built his life on sand was a one-time follower.

This discussion raises the question of what went wrong for one man who followed Jesus, heard His teaching, performed miracles in His name, but ultimately winds up in hell? It is clear in Scripture that Judas fulfils a God-ordained destiny and that this destiny is freely chosen. We may have a philosophical problem with this, but such tensions are part of the Bible and we needn't become too wound up by it. Judas is a stark reminder to us that however high the quality of coaching we receive, from Jesus, or from human leaders, we need to continue to obey. We limit God when we prefer our will to His, and if this is a permanent state of affairs, as opposed to part of the natural ongoing struggle, then we need to ask how serious we are about our faith in Christ. God's commands are always for our good. His words are life and we'd better believe it.

6. Remaining in unbelief

Unbelief is different from disobedience. When we are disobedient, we know what we should do but don't do it. When we are unbelieving we don't believe that what God says is really true. Jesus had to rebuke the Twelve for their lack of faith (Mark 4:40), and says to the two on the road to Emmaus, '… how slow of heart to believe all that the prophets have spoken' (Luke 24:25). John said that his Gospel was written that we might believe (go on believing) that Jesus is the Son of God and that by believing we might have life in His name. As we progress as followers, we will find our faith grow, just as the Twelve did.

When unbelief is a state of mind about all the Word of God, then this indicates that the person is not following Jesus at all. In many cases unbelief will come from ignorance not choice. People honestly acknowledge that they struggle. They want to follow Jesus, but for one reason or another haven't grasped the bigness of God and what He can do. They cry with the man whose son was tormented by a demon. 'I do believe; help me overcome my unbelief!' (Mark 9:24). The answer is not to force them to believe regardless, but to study God's Word so that there is understanding from which faith will flow. I may not believe that a friend's car is able to travel at 100 mph, but if I am in it and it happens, my unbelief disappears. God gives us a framework of Himself and His work in the world that makes faith in stuff we can't test reasonable, even if we can't quantify it. Study of His Word, interaction with Him in prayer, and conversation with older or more mature believers will often deal with unbelief very speedily. However, if church leaders insist on forcing people to accept God's Word before they are ready, it can only lead to heartache and disillusionment on the part of the follower.

7. Mixing with the wrong Christians

It can be fascinating to spend time with a family and note how the siblings ape their parents. It is not just mannerisms, but the worldview they adopt. Sometimes you find the outlook is diametrically opposite, but more usually you will find similarities are stark. Negative parents have negative children. Joyful, positive parents generally have children that are soaked in joy. Jesus spoke in similar terms about the effect that groups can have on an individual. He said of the Pharisees that they were more concerned with the praise of men than that which comes from God. He warned the disciples about the yeast of the Pharisees, who say one thing and do another (Mark 8:15). Such people will affect you if you let them. There is no doubt that the people we spend our time with can be a hindrance to spiritual growth. We may spend significant time in prayer and Bible study but the influences of others who also follow Jesus will also be factored in. If you regularly meet with people who are lacklustre about the new kind of life that Jesus offers, then it is very likely that you will become like them. Churches filter the teaching of Jesus through their own mindsets, for better or for worse, and it can be hard to buck the trend when your whole church views the kingdom one way.

If there are reasons why you are committed to a church that seems to you to be lacklustre (and of course you may be wrong), then remember that there are ways to feed yourself. Take responsibility for your own growth. Independency from your local church is a dangerous thing, but the average local church does not cater for the equipping of its members sufficiently for you to leave it up to them – that's why they remain average! You can listen to talks via the Internet (some are available free), tapes, MP3, video and Christian radio. You may have access to Christian TV. You can give yourself a reading schedule, mixing Bible and books aiding understanding of passages and themes. There are parachurch groups that put on conferences and local events that include input that will stretch your thinking and understanding of the new kind of life. I would caution you to check out your choices with an older believer. I have had the privilege of good teaching from some excellent churches and one of the finest Bible colleges but reading good books and listening to tapes has had an equal bearing on my spiritual growth.

What Jesus doesn't say

Jesus never promises that we will reach a stage in our Christian development where we can say that we have arrived. We should be able to say goodbye to some practices as Christ trains us, but we never reach the point where we don't need His daily help. But praise God, He doesn't give up on us when we face hindrances to growth – He can even make our Achilles heel a point of strength.

Main points
- Despite Christ's teaching and gift of the Spirit there are times when we will fail to grow.
- Christ has anticipated this and explains the reason and what we can do to prevent it.
- We never reach the point when we can say we have arrived, but with Christ's help we continue to advance.

ACTIONS

1. Recognise and deal with any of the factors that are preventing you from growing. Don't delay. Put a deadline on it and make yourself accountable to someone who can check that you have done it.
2. Consider whether Judas represents a failure for Jesus?
3. Do you know anyone who seems to be drifting? What can you do to help?

Note

1. D.A. Carson, *Expositor's Bible Commentary* Volume 8 (Zondervan, 1984).

Chapter 10

Most prayer never goes further than the ceiling

I said, 'Any chance of your phone number so I could stay in touch?'

She said, 'Sure', and quoted her number while I wrote it down.

To her, it was a casual question from the team leader of the summer outreach to international students. For me it was a desire to stay in touch with a girl I didn't want to say goodbye to, but as a team leader, hadn't felt comfortable in saying so.

Asking for a date is a risky business. You agonise. Does she want to go out with me? What if she is embarrassed by the question? You want to be in touch but what if she doesn't? I had no idea that the woman in question was actually delighted to keep in touch. Eight months later we were engaged to be married.

Much prayer is spoken without any expectation that there is anyone truly listening. How many mouth 'the Lord's Prayer' at school or public functions, doubting that there is any Father in heaven and that if there is, that He would be at all interested in staying in touch. Their words are spoken to the ceiling and the exercise is largely meaningless. It's very sad because of all the elements that make up our coaching experience, the time spent speaking with the Coach is perhaps the most fundamental. Many of those who mouth prayers, badly need His help.

Throughout the Bible, prayer is depicted as a real interactive relationship with God. It is not a ritual, or a mechanism activity where we 'get what we want', but the honest and genuine interaction between a person and God, made possible through Jesus and given life by the Holy Spirit. One of the most helpful summaries of the role of prayer in the life of the disciple I have read is that prayer is 'talking to God about what we are doing together'.[1] The definition steers us away from the two dangerous assumptions we can make about prayer: that our concerns don't register on God's radar, or that He is like a waiter waiting when we click our fingers. Our concerns are our concerns, real and present and thus brought to God in honesty. We know He has the right to decide what to do as He moulds our wishes into His desire that we learn as His follower, in the new kind of life He offers.

That the disciples needed to grow in their understanding and appreciation of prayer is evident from their observation of Jesus praying. 'Teach us to pray,' they said. As Jews, they would have prayed from youth. But there was something special about seeing Jesus interacting with His Father within the kingdom He was both living in and bringing to the lives of all who would follow Him. Jesus replies by giving them what is known as the Lord's Prayer, which is actually a model prayer that is rarely understood because it is wrenched out of the context of the new kind of life that Jesus invites us to.

So what does our Coach say about the way we should pray in the prayer He taught the Twelve?

1. Approach God as Father

Our approach to God as Father is no surprise for those familiar with what we call 'the Lord's Prayer', but a great shock to Jews used to thinking of God in certain ways. They were familiar with God's holiness, His otherness, His justice and His righteousness. Using the word 'Father' would be like us suddenly being allowed to call a member of the monarchy our friend. It would feel odd, even though we might (depending on our view of the monarchy) like the idea. Jesus wanted to delight the Twelve with a picture of God as a Father, with love, compassion, discipline and concern that His children might grow up and develop.

It is ironic that the next phrase in the Lord's Prayer takes our minds in the opposite direction to the one Jesus intended. 'Our Father who is in heaven', conjures up an image of a distant deity in a place different from us because of the way we understand 'heaven'. The stressing of God's otherness is an important aspect of Christianity but this is not the intention of Jesus here. In the thinking of the day, the world was split into three heavens. The Greek, unlike our English translations, uses the plural, 'heavens'. The words literally translated 'who is in the heavens' was intended to convey God's nearness, God 'who is in the atmosphere'. God is not identified with the air around, but He is that close. The phrase is not dissimilar to one used by the apostle Paul who tells the Athenians to call out to God for 'he is not far from each one of us' (Acts 17:27).

God is close; you don't need to summon Him. He is an unseen spirit of course; Jesus is not identifying God with any physical object or saying God is within you in a New Age understanding. Jesus is saying that prayer can properly be uttered anywhere. There are no special places – cathedrals and churches may aid prayers in focusing upon God, but there is nothing intrinsically holy about them. Jesus reminds us that He hears and answers us anywhere we may choose. He is keen that nothing should stop us from engaging in an ongoing conversation with God that involves Him in everything we do. Those who know Jesus, need never think that our prayer is not going further than the ceiling, for He is right there with us.

2. Don't be afraid to ask

List the uses of the word 'prayer' in the New Testament and you find that in the overwhelming majority of cases the person praying asks God for something. It's no surprise if, as we read the Bible, discover what Christ and the life He calls us to is like, we realise that we can't hope to enter this life without the ongoing work of God. To ask means to admit a need, sometimes to express our vulnerability or dependence. This is necessary in our human relationships and especially in our relationship with God.

A preoccupation with a self-focus is an unhealthy thing and the corresponding prayer life can be an excuse to be self-indulgent. But do note that the Lord's Prayer specifically commands believers to pray for themselves, albeit in the context of a community of believers: 'give us', 'forgive us', 'lead us'. Furthermore, many of Jesus' commands presuppose an acceptance that we are deficient. 'Come to me, all you who are weary and burdened' (Matt. 11:28); 'If anyone is thirsty, let him come to me and drink' (John 7:37); 'Then you will know the truth, and the truth will set you free' (John 8:32). A failure to ask for personal help actually serves to immobilise people and in being impoverished ensures that they are unable to ever look away from themselves. Not asking for yourself is ultimately selfish.

This asking feature of prayer is also emphasised outside the Lord's Prayer. In Luke we are told that the parable of the unjust judge was told so they would keep praying and not give up (Luke 18:1). Unfortunately some have misinterpreted the parable as teaching that you need to pester God like the widow pestered the judge. Whereas the point is that if a judge who is evil eventually gives the woman what she wants, how much more will God give what we need!

Persistence in prayer is not of course suggesting a formula whereby we eventually get what we want. As we interact with God we may have our mind changed, especially when our original wish is not granted. We discover that God has better answers, or wants to teach us things in waiting that we couldn't have picked up any other way. Prayer is not like an Internet chat room where we always receive instant replies if someone else is on line; though as we grow in understanding we will learn to discern the insights we receive as being from Him. Nevertheless, persistent prayer is good. We needn't feel that we are lacking in faith when we pray repeatedly.

3. Make sure you ask nicely

But requesting is different from demanding. A demanding spirit that insists on its way is the opposite to the spirit of prayer in the Bible. Answers to prayer, and indeed God's response to our reminding Him of His promises, always have a relational base. God owes us nothing. Anything we receive is by grace and comes out of the richness of His love. So we may know that God is gracious and that if we ask for bread He won't give us a stone, but that doesn't mean we can presume on His grace.

(a) Ask for daily needs

The encouragement to request daily bread reminds us of our utter dependence on God's provision. No food for a day means most of us are unable to function comfortably. We are built to be sustained daily. This prayer reminds the follower that all things come ultimately from God. This line of the prayer recognises this, even if for us the provision of daily bread is via a salary, loan, giro cheque or meal ticket.

(b) Ask for forgiveness

Jesus' teaching on forgiveness is central to the gospel. Within the Lord's Prayer the command is simple, we ask God to forgive us our sins. God is our Father, but there is an essential distinction between Him and us. He is holy and we are not. Our approach to Him in prayer, while welcomed, is in the context of forgiveness by God, a forgiveness that the disciples would understand can come because Jesus has died in the place of those who put their trust in Him.

The second part of the verse is crucial: 'forgive us our sins as we forgive those who sin against us'. Those who don't forgive others show by their actions that they haven't understood fully the nature of God's forgiveness of them. If they are hard hearted to people who have wronged them, they haven't appreciated the depth of their own rebellion and the greatness of the mercy extended towards them.

(c) Ask for protection in testing times

Jesus reminds us of the reality of the unseen evil forces and the old life within that can tug at us. We shouldn't be so confident about our walk with Christ that we think this prayer is redundant. We need God's daily involvement in our lives. The New Testament does not overplay the significance of the demonic realm. In the main we are exhorted to deal with evil in our lives, not to blame the evil forces. However, they are very real and Jesus promises to stand with us as we resist them. When we wonder whether God answers our prayers, this part of the Lord's Prayer reminds us that we may never know when the Lord has delivered us from evil. God saves us from situations we know nothing about. Part of our relationship with God is acknowledging His grace, not just in helping us through tough situations that we can see, but also keeping us away from others.

That doesn't mean that we are to be passive. Jesus tells His disciples to 'watch and pray' that they be not led into temptation. Under the new kind of life we are learning to get the point where sin doesn't have its enticing power, but meanwhile we are foolish to put ourselves in the way of temptation.

What Jesus didn't say

If we wrench the Lord's Prayer out of its context it loses its impact. Can we acknowledge that God is 'hallowed' without making sure that we know God's cleansing before we approach Him? Can we really pray 'Your kingdom come, your will be done', if we aren't prepared to allow it to come in our lives? We take care not to utter the words of the prayer with hypocrisy and deceit never intending to practise them.

Main points
- Prayer is talking to God about what we are doing together.
- We need to be clear that God is our Father and interested in us.
- Asking is a key part of our prayer life, and it's selfish not to.

Action
1. If familiarity with the Lord's Prayer has made it dull, try to put it in your own words. How could it be so simple that a child would understand it?
2. Choose a part of the prayer that you struggle to grasp most and ask Christian friends to tell you what they make of it. If you are still none the wiser, try a Bible commentary, or a minister.
3. Are there things you could be asking God for, but haven't; for example, grace to face a crisis? Wisdom to make a decision?

Note

1. Dallas Willard, *The Divine Conspiracy* (Zondervan, 1988).

Chapter 11

It's good to talk to Jesus

Here's a tip. If you want to get through to a real person when you phone a big company, don't, whatever you do, press the star key on your touch-tone phone when prompted to by that, oh so nice voice. The voice says that pressing various keys is 'to route your call more smoothly', but the truth is that it can take forever. I think the record for keys I have had to press is five. Instead, if you pretend you don't have a star key it means you get to a receptionist who puts you through manually. So now you know.

Having noted in the last chapter that talking with the Coach is one of the most important activities we can engage in, it has to be said that Christians struggle with prayer more than anything else. If you want to make a Christian feel guilty, (not that you'd want to …) ask them about their prayer life. We know we ought to pray more often and when we do we are glad we did, but somehow we never seem to get around to doing enough of it. One survey of ministers suggested that even those set aside for Bible teaching and church leadership struggle – on average they managed just seven minutes a day. Maybe we face the spiritual equivalent of the slow phone call – we need a tip to get through?

In fact, contrary to books and conferences that may claim to sell you their 'secret' – there's no mystery to prayer. Our Coach is happy to talk any time and any place. No star keys. If you find you struggle, here's what He is saying:

1. Tell me what's up

Our Coach reminds us that prayer is talking with Him about our life together. So it's clear there is nothing that can be outside the scope of our conversation. Some assume that if they are interested in what they pray about there must be something wrong. But there's no particular merit in choosing the obscure but worthy, if we would find reading the phone directory more fun. You will find of course that as your relationship with Jesus grows, you will find that your interest in what He's interested in will develop, so that your prayer net widens. We may be bolder in some cases than others; believing perhaps that a promise in the Bible applies to us or that God has given us particular faith to ask for something. Jesus says that if we have faith the size of a mustard seed we can tell mountains to move, ie nothing is impossible even if our faith seems small.

2. Play your part

Be informed by what the Bible commands us to pray, but be aware too that Jesus is equally keen for us to make decisions ourselves. A loving father who receives a call from his 28-year-old son asking if he can spend £55 on a pair of trainers is not impressed by the request, fearing that he hasn't allowed his son to develop appropriate independence. There are a whole host of things where the Bible makes no comment and leaves us free to choose. We may commit the situation to God and ask Him to involve Himself if He chooses to, but be free to exercise the liberty as independent beings to get on and make a decision. It is God's intention that we learn as His followers how He would live and act if He were in our position. Jesus is coaching us, not just so we can appropriately represent Him on earth, but also so we can be fitted for the new heavens and earth, where greater responsibility will be given. So it may be that as you pray, God is encouraging you to get on with what He has already said in His Word.

3. Trust God

Prayer is, at one level, an unnatural activity. We talk to someone we can't see and there's no prayer screen that can acknowledge that our prayer has been logged and will be dealt with as soon as possible. Prayer is thus an indication of where I put my confidence. Am I prepared to leave a situation with God, even when I don't see His answer or can't imagine how He will answer? There are many occasions in life when we may feel that we 'are only praying'. In leaving it to God we are doing the best thing possible and experience will prove that we have done the very best thing.

For the person who prays, waiting is a necessary part of the process. Many of the psalms echo the concerns and cries of people like us who wonder when God will act, while at the same time trusting Him to do so. As we wait we pray. Maybe there are things we should now do that were inappropriate when we began praying?

4. Be serious

If waiting can be hard work, many regard the practice of fasting even tougher. In simple terms, fasting is the denial of sustenance to achieve a spiritual objective. Jesus began His ministry with a 40-day fast and indicates that this was something He expected His followers to do, though not for that length of time. In the Sermon on the Mount He says: 'When you fast ...'

In John 4 He tells His disciples, who had gone off to buy food, 'My food ... is to do the will of him who sent me ...' (4:34) – a statement that can be taken metaphorically to indicate His satisfaction in obeying His Father's will, but more literally too. He told the devil in Matthew 4:4: 'Man does not live on bread alone, but on every word that comes from the mouth of God.'

At one level, fasting makes you feel uncomfortable. The denial of any necessity such as food will have that result. The danger is that we assume that there is merit before God in the discomfort, ie it's a super saint's activity. This feeds (forgive the pun) into the notion that the more unpleasant our faith, the more virtuous we are. But Christians who fast do so in order to focus more on God. The practice reminds them of their dependency and weakness and their need to look to God for the true sustenance they need. Many believers find it to be a practice that is spiritually uplifting and empowering. Our act of dependence on God serves to enable us to respond in a more focused way to His commands. Even those who don't make fasting a regular practice find it a great help when anticipating a major decision or activity where they are trusting God to help them. When Jesus' disciples struggled to expel a demon from a boy, Jesus said that this demon would only come out by prayer and fasting (according to some translations of Mark 9:29). Our ability to be used by God is raised when we fast. So Jesus' command to 'fast happily' in Matthew 6 isn't quite as strange as it sounds.

5. Look to bear fruit

Prayer is described as a key part of the character development. Jesus says, 'If you remain in me and my words remain in you, ask whatever you wish, and it will be given you. This is to my Father's glory, that you bear much fruit, showing yourselves to be my disciples' (John 15:7–8). The boldness of the promise comes as a surprise, but makes sense if we remain close to Christ. We remain close by reading His Word and so understanding the ways in which He works. Our desires slowly become united with His, so that we ask for the things that please Him and us.

If fruit is an obvious picture of character development (see Gal. 5:22–23) it is not the only thing. The implication of this passage is that there is a direct link between the impact of our lives and our prayer life. We can take this two ways – we can feel depressed that we don't pray more or we can be excited to think of the wider way that God is involved with us, and in the mystery of prayer able to do so much more. Certainly those who omit regular prayer from their life aren't intending to make any progress.

6. Spend time alone with God

In the Sermon on the Mount, Jesus contrasts the life of His followers with that of the religious leaders who made a spectacle out of their praying. We've seen already that the life of the believer starts from the inner life where Christ dwells. We resist the temptation to be deemed more spiritual or holy than we are by boosting our disciple ratings by displays of piety, preferring, as Jesus says, to pray in secret knowing that our heavenly Father sees what is done there and will reward us. The practice of secret prayer is a good test of our progress. It was Robert Murray McCheyne, the Minister of St Peter's Church, Dundee, in the early nineteenth century, who famously said, 'A man is what he is on his knees before God, and nothing more. Nothing more, nothing less.' You spend 20 minutes praying. No human being knows, but God does. He answers the prayer and rewards the prayer as He knows best, ironically in a deeper and more precious way than the show-off whose reward of being deemed 'religious' or 'holy' is momentary.

Jesus Himself practised this secret prayer, famously of course in His 40-day fast in the desert, but also at other times, choosing to be alone, sometimes in the hills. Secret prayer may sound more desirable to introverts than to extroverts, but for all it's a practice to incorporate. With secrecy comes silence. There is no command to be silent for any period of the day and for some the practice will be necessarily irregular, but when we are silent and on our own for a significant period, at least two hours, we will find the revs within our heart start to slow, and that it is easier to get in touch with God and ourselves. Both Jesus and the apostle Paul knew silence and secrecy at the beginning of their ministries; Jesus for 40 days, Paul in Arabia for an unspecified time (Gal. 1:17). It would be a surprise if you did not benefit.

7. Pray with others

The focus on silent and private prayer should not blind us to the fact that Jesus also advocated prayer with others. Indeed the plurals within the Lord's Prayer presuppose an awareness that our prayers join with those of the corporate community, even if we are praying on our own. Our prayer cannot be divorced from the local church community of which we are a part, which will give rise to prayer as we pray for one another, and about one another and become aware of our own failings in relationship with one another. Furthermore,

Jesus explicitly states that His Father will act on our behalf if we agree in prayer on a matter that is in line with His will and purposes. Corporate prayer can lead to the excesses of the Pharisees who love to be 'seen by men', as believers parade their theological knowledge, or even seek to influence church opinion. But the fact that others hear my prayers helps provide a check to idiosyncrasy, self-indulgence and sentiment. They also help those listening to learn from one another, encouraging increased faith and boldness. Jesus says He is present in a special way when two or three are gathered together in His name.

8. Extend God's kingdom

Our consideration of prayer would not be complete without a reminder that for the most part prayer must be seen as an offensive weapon. Many church prayer meetings are dominated by prayer for physical ailments, job situations, distressed people and the like – all legitimate and worthy objects of prayer. However, if we are failing to communicate with God on what He is doing in the world, then we are really missing out on the bigger picture and failing to 'talk about the things that concern us both'.

It has rightly been said that without prayer, we work, but with prayer God works. Jesus tells His disciples to pray to the Lord of the harvest to thrust out workers into the harvest fields. Christ-followers are aware that their effectiveness depends in no small measure on their prayer. Indeed they may be the only person who has ever prayed for a friend, colleague or family member on a regular basis.

What Jesus didn't say

In Jesus' teaching there is a lack of specific direction regarding daily devotions; the daily quiet time, involving prayer and Bible reading, journalling, practising solitude, fasting. Jesus never promotes one way above any other and offers no details beyond the general. We don't know how long He spent in prayer, which scriptures He had memorised, how long times of solitude lasted. He urges us to love God, love our neighbour and make disciples of all nations; so with this broad focus, it is up to us to find God-honouring ways to make sure we stay on track, given the general guidance He provides. All of which means that anyone who tries to lay on you any super duper method, hasn't been reading Jesus carefully. Use it if you wish, or abandon if you prefer. Jesus really doesn't mind. But make sure you do something.

MAIN POINTS
- There's no special secret to talking to God.
- Prayer shows our trust and our seriousness.
- Our fruitfulness flows from prayer.
- We should pray alone and with others.

ACTION
1. Don't assume that the routine you use will keep you interested without being changed. Variety is a great help. Use CDs, tapes, write out your prayers, pray with others, speak out your prayers, pray as you walk – anything to wake you out of your slumber.
2. Are there things you have never spoken to God about? What about your hobby, your pet hates, your favourite foods, your fears? Maybe your prayer life has become boring because you have limited the subjects you talk about?

PART THREE

Strengthen Vital Areas

The progressive involvement in the new kind of life means that we will become more like Christ from the inside out as our whole being is permeated with the life of God.

Each part of the self is progressively changed, and although we change as whole people, it is helpful to look at each part and how we co-operate with what the Spirit is doing.

God is seeking hearts (or wills) that naturally choose the pathways of the new kind of life, but He doesn't start there. First our thoughts need to be transformed, then in turn our feelings, for so many of our choices are essentially feeling-based. Then finally, our will, as we know what Christ wants us to do, feel good about that choice and are enabled to do it.

Our bodies and souls are also part of the process. The body can resist the changes we intend if it is not brought into line. Our soul, though not affected directly by us, is a vital part of the self that God also restores.

Chapter 12

Ideas change your world

Self-help is a growth industry. Enter any major bookshop and you will find a vast array of titles, many of which will be among the highest selling of any in the shop. The authors generally focus on the way people think, encouraging the reader with such phrases as: 'imagine your future'; 'see yourself differently'; 'create a vision for yourself'. The mind is regarded as a tool at our disposal to use to our advantage to be the person we want to be. The authors of the books are not being original. Our natural bent is to assume that we have to find 'life' ourselves – we construct belief systems that tell us that we are the source of our happiness and the reason we do not succeed. But we fail in the same way as Adam and Eve in the garden. If we are independent of God there is no help for us. We are like a diesel car being fed water.

Thoughts first

God has so designed us that our thoughts are a controlling factor in our lives. From the time that the serpent in the garden said to Eve, 'Did God really say you could not eat of any tree?' the path of spiritual transformation has been a battle of ideas: God's words versus a myriad of others. When it comes to spiritual change, it is no surprise that Christ starts with our thinking. Your first awareness of God came with a thought, as you heard the information about

Him in the gospel. You became aware that the world in which you live is a place created by God who loves you and sent His Son to die for you. That knowledge may not have created change in you the first time you heard it, but it was a necessary start. Exposure to the words about Jesus and His life eventually brought grief as you realised that you were in opposition to this love. You were convicted of sin, though at this point still distant from God. It is only when you decided to welcome God's Spirit (or Christ) into your life that you began to follow Him. You were enabled, as God worked with your spirit, to have new thoughts and feelings towards God and become involved in His life.

It's only then that we can think correctly about ourselves and our place in the world. Instead of being dependent upon self, we learn a dependence on God, choose to involve Him in life and learn to take appropriate action in the restoration of the world He has made.

It was following a succession of boyfriends that Mandy became a Christian. Convinced that the path to happiness lay through men, Mandy had gone from one guy to the next in search of someone who could make her feel special. She had bought into the lie promoted in every Hollywood romantic movie and confirmed, so she thought, by her parents' 24-year-old marriage with 'never a cross word'. But with each break up, the dream of marital bliss faded and it was at a time when she was 'definitely off men' that she was invited to church and discovered that the source of life and hope was in a different sort of relationship. With God fixed as her source of joy, she blossomed. Freed from the pain of disappointment, her relationships all round became less intense. She developed a heart for the disadvantaged in the community and found acts of mercy to the homeless natural and effortless.

God has designed us so that our thinking has a great effect on our feelings, even in people who put a high store on their emotions and gut instinct. I invariably find that a low mood is triggered by faulty thinking somewhere along the line. I get my head together and my feelings generally follow. Watch the two teams after the Oxford–Cambridge boat race. Both have expended equal amounts of energy – the margin of victory is often small, their bodies gasp for oxygen as lactic acid fills every pore. Yet one team feels elated, the other devastated because of their knowledge of victory and defeat and the value invested in this outcome.

Thinking also affects the choices we make. Unless I know who God is and what Christ has accomplished I will not choose to follow Him, however impassioned someone's plea that I do so. So, as a general rule, spiritual change means a change in my thinking first, then my feelings and choices (see Chapters 13 and 14).

So how does Christ want to change your thinking?

In computers we have default settings so that we don't have to select a font style, format and page layout every time we type a document. In the same way, our thinking has 'default settings' that need altering. We are locked into patterns developed over many years, which view the world and our place within it in a certain way. Sometimes these thoughts have been deeply held; images are so imprinted in our memories they become part of our internal architecture. God does not wipe clean the default settings when we come to faith. We need to patiently set and re-set them ourselves so that the new kind of life becomes the natural way we think. Remember the apostle Peter had been working with Jesus for three years when he was told, 'Get behind me, Satan! ... you do not have in mind the things of God ...' (Matt. 16:23). As we read our Coach's words we will continually discover that our thinking is awry. It takes humility to admit that 'we've got it wrong again', but bit by bit God rebuilds us so that we start to 'think God's thoughts after Him' and our instinctive 'reading' of life is informed by God and not the world around, or our 'natural intuition'. This book covers a number of areas where new ideas will change our world. Here are three areas to highlight.

1. Thinking about God

Jesus came to tell us that God can be trusted. All His teaching was based on the foundation of a God that cares deeply about us and always, without exception intends the very best for us. He notices us. He watches over us. If He chooses not to arrange a smooth path or intervene, it is for our good. It was A.W. Tozer who said that 'what comes into our minds when we think about God is the most important thing about us'.[1] We were made to enjoy God and be empowered by Him, but every time we believe a lie about Him we reduce the voltage. The self-help movement is absolutely right: our thinking is crucial. But they are dead wrong about the purpose of that thinking. Left to ourselves we will think ourselves into oblivion. So we learn to think of Him often, bringing Him into our day, conversing with Him in our minds as the day unfolds. The pastor, author, counsellor and founder of Crusade for World Revival (CWR), Selwyn Hughes, once told me of the Welsh businessman who, when facing a problem, would say to God, 'Now what should we do here?' Here was a man who was learning to let God shape his thinking.

When Jesus came He blew the minds of His followers. They began to realise who God is and how interested He was in them. I too learn that God loves me, cares for me, wants me to enjoy a new life and shun the old life. My vision of life is expanded. Before, I was confined to thinking my world was as small and narrow as what I could see and achieve. Now I am linked with God Himself – Creator of all that is, a God who is love and has plans and purposes for our world and us. It is extreme folly, though we all do it, to imagine that there is any part of the day or any activity in which we engage that couldn't benefit from an awareness of the presence of God.

2. Thinking about myself

In spiritual change you also need a right view of yourself. Earlier chapters have focused on our inbuilt bias away from God and the need for change. I will never stop needing to fight that as long as I live. However, alongside this thought, I remember I am made in God's image. It does God no credit if I diminish my importance and value. I don't exalt God by reducing myself, quite the opposite. Christ affirms that we are bearers of the image of God, resembling Him in His essential characteristics as a relational, emotional, choosing being. Christ gives me dignity. He calls me to follow Him and gives me real responsibility. I am dependent upon Him, but develop interdependence as He calls me to make choices that further His kingdom. The new kind of life I live is one I live; I am not a passive object jerked this way and that by a divine being bent on having His way irrespective of my involvement. He begins to trust me to launch into the adventure of seeing His will done as the new kind of life takes birth in others, and His power over evil is seen.

3. Thinking about change

The way we expect to change needs to change. I change as I hear the words of Jesus and agree with them, acknowledging their authority. Then and only then do I go on to act. When Jesus neared the end of His earthly life He asked that His Father would continue to transform His disciples: 'Sanctify them by the truth; your word is truth' (John 17:17). On another occasion many who had followed Him chose to leave. He turned to the Twelve and asked if they were going to leave as well. Peter said: 'Lord, to whom shall we go? You have the words of eternal life' (John 6:68). They knew there was nowhere else to turn. This was the best teaching around. This was the place to stay for mind transformation.

Take a simple example of change. Imagine you are on a diet and want to lose 10 pounds. The diet majors on choosing carbohydrates with a low glycaemic index. These foods are said to have a less drastic effect on blood sugar levels which helps stop food cravings and limits the deposit of fat. You have a vision for a slimmer you and change your thinking about certain foods. This enables you to choose one type of food over the other. Your will power is thus radically affected by your vision of change and trust in the means of changing. Two things will prevent this working. If your vision of a slimmer you diminishes, or you believe the diet doesn't work.

When it comes to our spiritual change, we may try to do what we believe God wants before we have actually become convinced in our minds that this is the path we want to follow. God says 'be reconciled with your brother' so we attempt to mouth words of apology, without having first become convinced in our minds that God's command is one we want to follow. In truth we feel aggrieved and rather enjoy feeling that we are the martyr who is justly angry with our brother. We need to work on our thinking, understand that we are living a new kind of life, that God in Christ has forgiven us much worse and so we can be free to be generous to all who have 'sinned against us'.

Take any command of Jesus and you will find a 'thinking' component. Jesus knows that if your thinking isn't changed, you will not be truly willing to do what He asks. Ultimately it is His overarching vision of life with God at the helm, providing us with all that we need that frees us to live the life He intends.

Give it time

You may be intimidated by the thought of thinking like Jesus thought. But ask yourself this: 'Has my thinking changed since I became a Christian?' If the answer is 'yes' as I trust it is, then why is it so hard for you to imagine that other thoughts can change? As you soak yourself in the Word of God, the way you think will change. And as you focus on what Jesus calls you to do in this book, you will start to think like Him

WHAT JESUS DIDN'T SAY

Jesus didn't say that the Christian life was just about having correct thoughts. If that's where it stays we have problems. The saying, 'it's the thought that counts' is not true in this case. Thinking is the start of godly living, but it needs to lead to action. Jesus said that it was those who did the will of God who were wise (Matt. 7:24). The classroom for His coaching of the Twelve was real life with real people and real needs. As total people, thinking leads to appropriate feeling and appropriate action. It is not an end in itself, which is maybe why it has received such a bad press.

As we have hinted already, thinking does not mean being intellectual. An illiterate person who knows and understands the gospel is thinking more clearly and with greater profit than the university professor who chooses to trust in his or her own wisdom. Making Christians think is a healthy, godly activity because it is a God-given means of change. Think about it.

MAIN POINTS

- Christ starts His coaching by changing our thoughts.
- His Word provides the understanding of who God is, who we are in relation with and how change takes place.
- We are enabled to change by the Spirit's work applying God's Word and enabling our minds to come alive.

ACTION

1. Consider the areas of your life, which you suspect Jesus is keen to coach you on. How has your thinking affected your behaviour in these areas?
2. Do you see Jesus as intelligent? Start acknowledging that there's nothing in your professional or personal life that He can't help you with. Start asking His advice.
3. Spend some time reading the Gospels. Choose to focus on some of Jesus' teaching. Read it repeatedly and ask how His ideas differ from yours.

Note

1. A.W. Tozer, *The Knowledge of the Holy* (Harper Collins, 1985).

Chapter 13

Feelings are good servants but lousy masters

Being rejected for a job I have been interviewed for has happened to me a few times. I turned one down myself when I discovered the small print required me to work night and day for the company, and with two others, there were better opportunities just round the corner. But one job I went for I thought was as good as mine – there were too many coincidences for me not to think that God was in it. The job had come to me out of the blue when I was praying about a change, and the more I learned about it, the more suited I seemed. If you had asked me to stake my house on it I would have done. The interview went pretty well and I settled down to receive the written confirmation. I can still recall the emotions on finding the rejection letter in my mailbox one morning. 'I am sorry to inform you that you haven't been successful in the interview for ...' it began. 'I imagine this must be a disappointment for you ...' Disappointed? No. Try gutted, shell-shocked, devastated. I could not believe it. The job was mine and the reasons they gave for not offering it didn't even make sense.

God has made us to feel – every last one of us. The emotions may be hidden, they may be suppressed, they may have been managed by our response to parents who squashed us, or a belief that it is not appropriate to get 'emotional'. But we still have them. Indeed we live at a time when it is normal to expect our feelings to be satisfied, if we are to be 'true to ourselves'. People are told: 'Go with your heart.' If we are upset with someone we are encouraged to sort them out: 'Don't get mad, get even' is the motto. For many people, feelings of joy, anxiety, confidence, uncertainty, joy, apathy, terror, can dominate to the point that they colour everything else.

When we begin to follow Christ we will find that our emotional life does not automatically do what we might hope it would do. We still lose our temper, get hacked off with poor driving, loathe the fact that Aunt Agatha has come to stay, become envious of someone who has what we want. We know that a person dominated by how they feel is at the constant mercy of those feelings and behaves accordingly, but we know this includes us. Sometimes we battle to paper over the emotional cracks yet we know that becoming like Jesus includes an enjoyment of a new kind of life. So how do we grow to feel like Jesus felt, with appropriate emotional response at appropriate times?

1. Understand your emotions

First we need to analyse the types of emotions we have. This isn't at all easy. Our emotions are so much part of us that they characterise who we are and how we are going to behave. If someone is moody, we know to tread carefully. Someone 'in love' may be more pleasant to be around. Emotions can be deceptive: we can feel marvellous, yet behave dreadfully. When they come knocking at our door we need to pause and check their ID before welcoming them in. We need help to get a handle on what they are and how they change. Larry Crabb writes of the distinction between, on the one hand, pleasant and unpleasant emotions, and on the other, constructive and destructive ones.[1]

For example, if we lose a job we love we will experience unpleasant emotions (disappointment, rejection, shock). If we then find a better job we feel pleasant emotions (joy, acceptance, relief). Whether a Christian or not we will feel what we feel. Christians who immediately laugh off the disappointment of the job loss are lying to themselves and to others. Life hurts and being a Christian is no security blanket.

But we then need to ask whether this emotion is moving us towards God or away from God. Whether or not the emotion is nice does not dictate how we are responding spiritually. So it is conceivable that the unpleasant emotion of losing a job could be constructive – our experience of sadness drives us to God. It is also possible that the pleasant emotion of securing a job could be destructive – we become proud that we are snapped up so soon and forget to acknowledge God's involvement. So, regardless of whether the event causing emotions is pleasant or not, it's our response that matters to our Coach. Emotions are a bit like the warning lights on the car dashboard. If you ignore one, it could be problems ahead for the engine. Is this emotion just a part of life's rich tapestry, or is our response indicating a need for a look under the bonnet? Our feelings are one of the major ways that Satan trips us up – so if you think you need to take a look, do so.

2. Changing emotions

Understanding emotions will help us learn how to change them too. If we find that our emotions are destructive we need to ask what is taking place within us. As we have noted, feelings can be very hard to identify. They are personal to us and we generally feel that we have a right to them. Mature people, and especially mature believers, disentangle themselves from the emotion and say, 'OK this is how I feel, but that doesn't mean I need to act on it.' They ask: 'What is the root of this pain? What wrong thinking or beliefs are causing it?'

Reflecting on the job I thought I was ideal for, my reaction to the rejection letter was more than mere 'disappointment' (unpleasant emotion) but had become anger (destructive emotions) that those interviewing hadn't agreed that this was God's will! It took me a while to realise that my reaction revealed a move away from God. Instead of accepting His wise purposes, I had effectively been demanding that it turn out the way I wanted it to. The solution was to acknowledge to God that I was trying to do His job for Him, apologise to Him and ask His forgiveness. I found as I started thanking Him for His grace and love and overruling, the anger subsided. There will be a myriad of emotions which we face that will have little effect on us and say nothing about us – this is not an invitation to get introspective when we burn the toast, or are late for an appointment. But in some cases an internal look will move us forward in a way that the mere suppression of emotions would not.

3. Replacing emotions

We can change emotions by changing our thinking, but Christ's long-term goal is that we replace our feelings so they become the sort He would have. It is all very well for me to change from feeling anger at not getting a job, but far better not to have got angry in the first place.

As we read and accept the truth of His coaching, our thoughts are brought in line with God's, and together with our body, soul and will (which we look at in the next chapters) our emotions will start to change. In John 7:37, Jesus says, 'If anyone is thirsty, let him come to me and drink.' Thirst implies a longing, a feeling of desperation, of need, of emptiness. But His answer is to focus on Him; to talk to Him, bring our lives to all He is. We read, 'Whoever believes in me [puts his confidence in me], as the Scripture has said, streams of living water will flow from within him.' As we trust and look to Him, our feelings will change as we experience God's Spirit at work. Jesus wants us to know the feelings of love, joy and peace, and the rest of the fruit of the Spirit that Paul outlines in his Galatians letter (Gal. 5:22). A life that is full of the love of God doesn't have time for the many negative and self-focused emotions that could fill our lives.

In a book this size there is little space for looking at the more complex aspects. I recognise that describing how thinking changes feelings may seem simplistic especially if you know people who struggle with depression or mental illness, and seem incapable of the sort of changes in mindset that I am advocating. There are medical conditions that require careful handling, medication, counselling or therapy. The Spirit doesn't change our feelings with a click of the fingers. Furthermore, all of us experience feelings that have become embedded within us that run on the old programs developed through childhood and on into adult life. It's as if our DNA has been tampered with by events that cause a 'reflex reaction'. Sometimes we aren't even aware that they are there, or that we exhibit that feeling and subsequent behaviour pattern. It was a long time before I realised that I had become a 'people-pleaser'. I had worked out that life is smoother when people like me, so I made the vow 'whatever you do, Andy, don't upset people'. This people-pleasing would colour my emotional life and make any declaration of a position that others disagree with impossible. God is working to change me from the inside, to prefer His approval to that of others.

But, given these riders about our feelings, thinking and emotions do go together. You are not at the mercy of your emotions. Your Coach wants you to understand them, change them and replace them so that your interior becomes like that of Christ whose reaction to every event was in keeping with His Father's concern that the new kind of life be seen and known.

What Jesus didn't say

Jesus never promised happiness. He promised a deep sense of joy, love from the Father and abundant hope based on the Father's promises, but not happiness as such. So don't worry about being happy. Look to God, have confidence in Him. Love Him and you will find that bit by bit an abiding joy will grow and you will wonder why the pursuit of happiness was such a big deal.

Main points

- We are emotional beings.
- We need to understand whether emotions are constructive or destructive.
- We can change emotions by identifying the roots in our thinking.
- Christ is looking to change us so that we feel the way He does about God, ourselves and the world.

Actions

1. For the next week make a conscious decision to acknowledge how you are feeling. At the end of each day note any dominant feelings. (These might include apathy, joy, anger, contentment,

fear, excitement, lacklustre.) What are they telling you? How has your thinking led to them?

2. If someone were to describe your typical emotional state, what would they say? How does this affect your ability to live as God is directing you? What helps and what hinders?

Note

1. See Larry Crabb, *Understanding People* (Marshall Pickering, 1988).

Chapter 14

Wise choices – a good habit to get into

A colleague who you find intensely irritating has taken a few days off sick, but the rest of the office knows that he is actually at the races. Office satire follows with suggestions about where the colleague might go next time he's sick. Do you join in?

Your work is rarely commended, but on this occasion you receive a 'well done' from someone that matters. But the part they commend is the part where you received help from someone else. Do you say something?

You are paying for your car service at the garage and you notice that the mechanic has failed to include the cost of a £45 part. The garage had been slow in completing the job and you had already decided not to use them again. What do you do?

It is not difficult for us to know what was the right thing to do in the above scenarios: you don't join in, you commend the person who helped you and you add the £45 to the bill. But what were you tempted to do?

1. First choice

Our choices are at the heart of what it means to be human, indeed as far as the Bible is concerned, the word 'heart' is the place where choices are made. We all have an independent will, which is spiritual in nature and makes decisions. We are the sum of all the choices that we have made or have been made for us. Our character has been formed according to our daily and regular choices. The role of our choices is pivotal in our starting with Christ. Aided by God's Spirit, we choose to follow Christ and deny ourselves because of the richness of living life in fellowship with God in His kingdom. This is not the choice of one who is faced with an unpalatable option and does so because he's told to, but the choice of one who recognises that life is found in God and this choice is the wisest he will ever make. As Rick Warren says in his book, *Purpose-Driven Life*, 'your commitments can develop you or they can destroy you, but either way, they will define you.'[1]

Having chosen Christ, we reaffirm that choice often. The Bible speaks of us 'taking up our cross' daily. We need to because our spirit (or will) has been shaped over the years and has preferences. Some of these are fine and become enhanced when we come to Christ, others reflect our old nature and need crucifying. There is no growth in Christ-likeness without this fundamental shift. So although I became a Christian at the age of seven, I have to continue to choose God's way; temptations come and there have been many times when I knew the right way and chose the wrong one, and times of procrastination when I knew the path I was on was unwise. No doubt your experience will be similar. The key thing is, do I want to want to follow? Do I want to be the sort of person who chooses God's way?

2. Maturing choice

We have deliberately looked at choosing after thinking and feeling because ultimately our choices are informed by our thinking and feeling. Our Coach is in the business of moving us to the point where choosing to live for God is literally second nature. It will take time (remember this is a lifelong process) but in spite of what some Christians seem to imply, He will not force us, manipulate us or cajole us. He is so changing our thinking and emotions that we naturally and joyfully choose to follow.

A man who longs for his daughter to enjoy playing the piano as much as he does receives little pleasure if she plays grudgingly because he has forced her. John Piper puts it like this: 'God is most glorified in us when we are most satisfied in him.'[2] The new kind of life is lived as we joyfully do what He says we should do. Christ's commands describe the new kind of life that we aspire to. They are not 'case law' that we slavishly obey, but the kind of life that people who have the inner life of Christ pulsing through their veins will naturally live. When I buy my wife flowers she hopes that it is out of love for her. If I told her that I was merely practising 'Hardaker's tips for wise husbands' she would be less than impressed. I might need tips from time to time of course, but the point is this, my relationship with her is such that the buying of flowers from time to time is a natural way of life that I joyfully engage in. In the same way our behaviour flows from within as Jesus seeks hearts that are changed. He reserves His severest criticism for the Pharisees who outwardly seemed pious but failed because their hearts were not for God. In Mark 7:21, when Jesus speaks with His disciples, He tells us that it is from the heart that evil comes. 'The good man brings good things out of the good stored up in his heart, and the evil man brings evil things out of the evil stored up in his heart. For out of the overflow of his heart his mouth speaks' (Luke 6:45). We typically judge the outward behaviour, God judges the heart from which the behaviour comes. He seeks worshippers in 'spirit and in truth', ie those that worship God from the heart where their spirit chooses to please God.

This means Christ wouldn't be content for us to merely exercise will power towards His ways, without engaging our thinking and feeling. He knows that appealing to the will is like asking a man with a broken leg to run a marathon. Instead he starts elsewhere. He works to transform our thoughts, our feelings and bodies alongside our hearts so that we become the kind of people who obey Him.

Imagine that you are in a job where you normally work Monday to Friday. Your boss asks you to work on a Saturday. Your job is OK, but not so great that you welcome the prospect of weekend work. You say, 'No I don't want to do it.' You might even feel slightly depressed at the prospect. You prefer a day off, to the overtime. What would make you want to change your mind? No amount of work on your will is likely to accomplish it. Your boss might lean on you heavily and prevail upon you to come in, but even if you did it would be against your will. Saturday work is out as far as you are concerned. But now imagine that your boss told you that if you worked on a Saturday you would receive a £2,000 bonus. How would you then think and feel? Tempted now? Of course, the new information causes you to change how you think and feel about your 'choice'. Faced with such a reward you might even sign up early for Saturday duty. Your feelings towards Saturday would change.

In the same way Jesus looks to so change the way we think that our feelings are changed and we joyfully choose to walk His way. Temptations that would drag us away in a moment have less power as we think like God and learn to focus on the new kind of life and not the seemingly alluring alternatives. So Jesus is seeking to bring us to the point where we not only do the right thing in the scenarios at the start of this chapter, it wouldn't occur to us to do anything else.

3. Choosing to choose

Whenever you read a command of Jesus and know that deep down you don't want to do it there are two things to do. The first is to deny yourself and do it anyway. Doing God's will even when we don't feel like it is always better than not doing it. But at the same time you go to Jesus and tell Him that this is how you feel about it. Your reaction to the command shows that there's room for some work. You will find that somewhere along the line you are believing a lie about where life lies. It never lies outside God's revealed will. Believing this lie, your will believes at that moment that the best course for you is not God's way. So you need to tackle the lie, change the way you think and prayerfully look to God to help you want what He wants. If you don't do this reasoning, you will end up operating out of sheer will power, your mind will be unconvinced and the next time the temptation comes you will be back to square one. But if you work on your thinking, and ask for God's help, you will be surprised how quickly you reach the point where the same temptation does not even register with you.

4. Forced choices?

It is worth adding at this point that our actions are always a result of our choices (assuming a healthy person) even if we are not aware why we have acted as we did. When we act in ways that we don't understand, we may wonder why, asking ourselves, 'What came over me?' There will be a reason. This seemingly irrational action may be because of something that happened in the past. We chose to shield ourselves from pain and vowed in our hearts that this would never happen to us. Sometimes we fool ourselves that the behaviour is irrational because we are not prepared to face what is really going on. If you are conscious of this behaviour, it is certainly worth chatting to a trained counsellor or wise leader who can help you isolate your motivation. This is not to pry into your private life, but to liberate you to make the free and joyful choices that God has always intended. God is looking to so change us that we willingly abandon ourselves to His will knowing it to be the sweetest most delightful course open to us. God is good and the new kind of life He promises is the one everyone would choose if they knew God the way Jesus does. Self-denial is the very best way to live. We can at last relax for perhaps the first time in our lives.

WHAT JESUS DOESN'T SAY

The belief that we can be good Christians by will power alone is ingrained within many church cultures. Preachers appeal to the will, without going through the mind so that congregations know what to do, but not why or how. If you are self-disciplined and reasonably together you can probably make a good attempt at being a good Christian on the surface but ultimately your life with Christ will lack passion because deep down you will know that it is you and not God that is keeping your spiritual show on the road. This style of Christianity is at a loss when it comes across areas the Bible has little or nothing to say about. Jesus looks for hearts that are so developed that they naturally and joyfully obey Him, with a passion that is continually amazed at the grace of God that has made this new kind of life possible.

MAIN POINTS

- Our choices are at the heart of who we are.
- Christ is bringing us to the point where we joyfully choose His way.
- What we choose is determined by our thinking and feeling when we come to choose.

ACTION

1. Consider the view that God wants to bring us to the point where He would empower us to do anything we want. Can you imagine God doing that with you? What would need to change?
2. Consider the areas where you know you don't want to do what you know you should, eg forgiving someone who has hurt you, speaking to a newcomer at church who seems odd, keeping calm when you are cut up on the road. How would you need to think differently about the situations so that you truly wanted to obey God?

Notes

1. Rick Warren, *Purpose-Driven Life* (Zondervan, 2002).
2. John Piper, *Desiring God* (IVP, 2002).

Chapter 15

Look after your body, where else would you live?

You don't have to appear regularly on a catwalk to be concerned about your body. We all are. We want to look our best, be healthy, feel good. We wouldn't want to be regarded vain, but a poor haircut or an extra stone can affect us. Like it or not we know we have to look after ourselves. It's a fact of life.

Despite its universal importance, I have listened to more than 3,500 talks on the Bible during my life, but not one on the body. This is not because of the dress sense of the men who address us (it is still mostly men) nor because the speakers might be embarrassed that they can't practise what they preach. It isn't that I avoided talks on the body because I feared what might be said. It's because in the minds of many Christian leaders the body is of little relevance, after all, they say, spiritual growth is not body building; an inappropriate focus on the body, sometimes called rather quaintly, 'our temporal needs', can obscure what God is doing.

However, the dividing off of spirit and body reflects a Greek mindset that has infected the Western Church. In God's eyes, all things were created good and are to be redeemed – body and spirit. Jesus took on human flesh and lived among us in a physical body. The Incarnation tells us that the body is something good. We can be grateful for the frame in which we were born, however much we may wish it were different.

But the failure to thank God for the body is not the major concern of our Coach. Jesus is concerned that our body does what it should in our spiritual growth. We can't divorce the body and the spirit (will) as if one acts independent of the other. Love for God and people is primarily expressed through that body. Jesus says we should love the Lord our God with all our 'strength', which comes at least in part from the body.

So, doing the will of God without concern for the body is like a Formula One racing driver furiously preparing race tactics and tuning the engine without giving thought to the design of the car's chassis. Our body is not an irrelevance but a vital part of life's race. We may intend to behave and live in certain ways but our body works against us. As Jesus said, 'The spirit is willing but the flesh [the body] is weak'.

For example:
- You look with disgust at someone you don't like.
- You find yourself instinctively flirting with people you find attractive.
- You grab at food or drink when you are hungry.
- You lash out when someone hurts you.
- You are too tired to do things God has asked of you.
- You 'must' have certain food, narcotics or alcohol.
- You are subject to mood swings that impair your judgment.

It is as if your body is your team – you have done the pre-match coaching; working on your tactics (thinking), your emotional responses (feeling), your decisions on the pitch (choosing), but if you don't work on the body it is as if all your pre-match preparation has gone out the window because, during the game, the body has a mind of its own. Research claims that when we communicate, just 7% of our communication is through the words we use, 38% through the tone of voice and a massive 55% through the way our body moves. It's not for nothing that we have coined the phrase 'body language'; we reveal, or conceal, or confuse by our body.

So what does a transformed body look like and how can we get one, and fast?

A transformed body is one that is poised to live as Jesus would. Jesus went through all the sensations that we go through. He was tired, hungry, thirsty, but His body was always under control so that it served the end of living for God. He was never a slave to His body the way we are.

We have already stressed in this book that if we deal with the inside the outside will follow, so we are not talking here of any false acting that in reality fools no one. No, this is my body being ready to live out the will of God on a daily basis.

Goodbye to the old ways

Our life before coming to Christ is lived around our needs. We think that we are free, but according to the apostle Paul, we are controlled by the sinful nature (Rom. 7:5). Made for community, we relate defensively, preferring the castle of our own thoughts and plans to God's broad and exciting kingdom. When we are being sensible we have a modicum of control over the body, but more often than not it calls the shots, demanding satiation of appetites, food, drink, sex, sleep, acquired taste for drugs – legal and otherwise.

When God places within us the seed of the new life, we start to look outward and our energy is turned towards following Christ. Our will wants to please Him and changes may come automatically. The body is less tense, the face smiles more, the head is lifted, when once it was bowed. But just as the spiritual choices we make are not automatic, so our body does not automatically behave as it should. Old habits mean that it wants to dominate still. The old addictions are still there; our sexual passions have not been neutered. The internal fight between good and evil is ever real. So for our body to respond to our thoughts and choices, rather than lead inappropriately, we will need to bring it into line.

What does our Coach advise?

S and S

Jesus coached His followers by example. His body had no natural advantage over ours. He had to train it to be available to serve. At the very start of His ministry when Jesus was led by the Spirit into the wilderness to be tempted by the devil, we read that He fasted for 40 days and 40 nights. This symbolised the 40 years of testing that the Israelites endured in the wilderness on their way to the promised land but it also teaches us the practical benefits of silence and solitude (S and S) – as well as fasting, but this isn't our point here. On other occasions He would get up early and head for the hills to pray (Mark 1:35). He urges his disciples to pray alone (Matt. 6:6).

He assumes that the Twelve would also fast (Matt. 6:17). We assume we have to give in to the body to be 'satisfied', fasting reminds us that we don't. During His ministry Jesus would go to the hills to pray on His own and get away from the crowds. Solitude and silence (S and S) are demonstrated to the Twelve, and commanded when He tells us to pray alone in our room.

Solitude and silence help us have bodies that are able to stand aside from the momentum and rush that characterises so many people's lives, and to learn to serve the purposes of the new kind of life. We deny ourselves the gifts of sound and company in order to give God the opportunity to draw near to us. Many down through the centuries have included solitude and silence as part of what have been called 'spiritual disciplines'; practices that we can perform ourselves that will enable us to live like Christ. They are not actions to gain merit with God, but ones that reflect a wise understanding of who we are, our susceptibility to temptation and a desire to sharpen the body for actions that please God.

F and F

If our body is not healthy it is difficult for us to accomplish what God requires of us without being preoccupied with our physical condition. Much illness cannot be avoided, but it makes sense to play our part in ensuring that we are able to accomplish what God calls us to do, especially if some of our Christian service is on top of a heavy daily workload, leading to late evenings and busy weekends. Jesus' itinerant lifestyle would have included a considerable amount of walking and if it would be impossible to prove that Jesus 'worked out' from the Gospel evidence, it is clear that He was a strong and sturdy guy; it was no wimp that overturned the money-changers' tables in the Temple precinct and many men died under the scourging He underwent prior to the cross.

So it is not stretching the Bible to argue that our Coach modelled a life of sensible 'food and fitness'. Would He not want us to focus on foods that nourish us without creating empty feelings and cravings two hours later? Some simple work on diet can do us the world of good. Dieticians recommend that we drink a minimum of two litres of water and have five portions of fruit and vegetables daily. Cutting down on saturated fats and avoiding excessive carbohydrates, will all help us maintain energy and alertness throughout the day. Jesus expects His followers to fast on occasions, and although the intention is that we might better focus on God and receive from Him, fasting has considerable physical benefits too, providing it is done sensibly. We can go too far; Jesus never lectures His disciples on diet, and a preoccupation with physical shape and looks is a definite distraction. But many Christians would be surprised to learn that what they thought was a spiritual problem, eg lethargy, was actually nothing more than a regular unwise choice of meals.

R and R

Rest and relaxation were also part of Jesus' routine. On one occasion He took His disciples away to spend time with them (Mark 6:31). Some of His times on Lake Galilee would have included rest and it's likely that the journeys to and from visits to towns and villages were low key. Jesus may have challenged the conventional understanding of what could be done on the Sabbath, but there is nothing to suggest that He did not value the day set aside for rest and reflection on God's goodness.

Again, we can go too far. Some Christians haven't discerned the difference between R and R and laziness. But many Christians would be surprised at how differently they would live if they had ample sleep and times focused on recuperation. When did you last spend a whole hour doing absolutely nothing? Is your life a struggle because you don't get enough rest? Is there someone who could take the children off your hands? Do you have to drive yourself so hard – after all who is God, you or God?

What Jesus didn't say

Jesus didn't say, neglect the body because you will ditch it. Our present skin won't last, but after the resurrection Jesus still had a body, albeit different to ours, and after death we too will enjoy a new life in a new body. The body is there to serve us. Making it smart and attractive for the outside world is different from the posturing and parading that can go on. Christians are not immune from judging people on the surface. Physical beauty can be admired and sought to a point, but true beauty is inward. A person whose physical attributes may not score 10 in a beauty contest has a radiance and vigour because God is there. And whatever else we have going for us, that is one attraction that everyone, ultimately needs and will come to value.

Main points

- The body is an integral part of our spiritual development.
- Christ aims that the body is ready to serve God's purposes.
- Silence and solitude, food and fitness, rest and relaxation, are all areas we need to consider as we co-operate in the life-transformation our Coach seeks for us.

Action

1. Spend some time alone in quiet. Consciously give your body to God. Thank Him for the bits you enjoy. Trust Him for the bits you don't. Tell Him you don't want it to hold back what He intends to do.
2. Consider your diet. Are there things you know you should cut out, or incorporate. What's stopping you?
3. Ask Him for grace to cope as years pass, or as illness afflicts you.
4. Value your body as His gift to you. Ask Him to allow you to put it into proper perspective.

Chapter 16

Looking after your soul as it looks after you

We have focused on those parts of the self that we can do something about: our thoughts, our feelings, our choices and our bodies. But there is another part that we need to be aware of, a part that is affected directly by God – the soul.

The soul is a bit like the hidden heating system in a large office block. It is foundational and affects everything: company employees would soon notice if it disappeared or malfunctioned. But on a day-to-day basis, it is not acknowledged, indeed you could probably work at the company for years without recognising it was there at all. Providing your work temperature is comfortable, why be concerned?

Dallas Willard looks at the biblical data on the soul and concludes:

> The soul is that aspect of your whole being that correlates, integrates and enlivens everything going on in the various dimensions of the self. It is the life centre of the human being. It regulates whatever is occurring in each of these dimensions and how they interact with each other and respond to surrounding events in the overall governance of your life. The soul is 'deep' in the sense of being basic or foundational and also in the sense that it lies almost totally beyond conscious awareness.[1]

If it 'lies almost beyond conscious awareness' we could argue that we have got on perfectly well without giving a lot of thought to the soul, so why bother now? But when Jesus told us to love God, we were told to love Him with all our soul. There are no parts, not even the deeper hidden parts, that can be left out. And most important, the soul will be that part of us that lives on beyond death, awaiting the new resurrection body at Christ's return. So it's good to become acquainted!

So here are six things our Coach wants you to grasp about your soul.

1. You have one

We have quoted Dallas Willard as saying that the soul is the life centre of the human being. This is in contrast to some modern thinking that people do not have a soul at all: they say, the non-physical aspect of our being is seen as chemical reactions in the brain. We are merely a collection of matter, and do not, indeed cannot, exist separately from the body. When we die, that's it.

The definition of the soul also stands against the recent trends that understand us to have a soul, but do not believe the God of the Bible provides the framework for it. Some people in the West, without any particular religious leanings, have found the materialistic approach to life bankrupt, and become interested in the idea of a soul, believing that we all need to pay attention to a deeper part of ourselves. We even have a bestselling book entitled *Chicken Soup for the Soul*. People are encouraged to find their soul mate – someone who clicks with them at a deeper level than physical attraction. But Jesus tells us that we are more than chemicals. We have a soul and He cares about it.

2. Christ saves the soul

In the Church, if the word soul is used at all, it has been traditionally associated with the spiritual side of a person, the part that God saves, when a person trusts Christ. Evangelists are referred to as 'soul winners' in some circles.

This is in part because Jesus Himself uses soul in this way to describe the part of man that goes on beyond this life: 'What good will it be for a man if he gains the whole world yet forfeits his soul?' (Matt. 16:26). A parable relates God's words to a man who had been too focused on his farming to prepare for eternity: 'This very night your life will be demanded from you' (Luke 12:20).

When we trust in Christ, we receive God's life within us. The psalmist says, 'he restores my soul' (Psa. 23:3). God works at the very deepest parts of our being by His Spirit so that our soul and our spirit are given life. We find ourselves in touch with God and His kingdom.

Jesus showed His awareness of soul weariness: 'Come to me, all you who are weary and burdened, and I will give you rest. Take my yoke upon me and learn from me, for I am gentle and humble in heart, and you will find rest for your souls' (Matt. 11:29). Jesus paints a glorious picture for people in Israel weary of trying to keep the seemingly endless number of laws, now finally finding rest in Him.

So, if the soul is like the heating in a building, becoming a Christian could be like an old building having a heating system renovated. Employees had become used to the cold building and dressed accordingly. The cold had become normal. Then the employees realised with the heating now working they could shed their overcoats and that it was now unusual to have to fight the cold. When Christ renovates the heart it brings a revolution to our whole being. Everything works better. The soul that unites and integrates life is enriched and refreshed by God's Spirit within the Christian's life. We realise how cold the old life was.

3. It is separate from your spirit

Christians disagree about whether we are body and soul/spirit, or body, soul and spirit. On balance, although spirit and soul are seemingly used interchangeably, they are different things. The human spirit is the form that our will takes within us, distinct from the soul. Perhaps the confusion between soul and spirit may come because soul is spiritual. You can't see it, or feel it, but just because it is spirit doesn't mean it can't be distinct from our spirit.

4. Your soul expresses itself

The soul is almost seen as a separate 'life' within us. Elsewhere in the Gospels we find that the word translated 'soul' expresses emotions such as grief (Matt. 26:38, AV); anguish (John 12:27, AV); exultation (Luke 1:46, AV); pleasure (Matt. 12:18, AV). Such emotions come from who we are. Jesus speaks of His own soul being distressed in the Garden of Gethsemane as He anticipates His death. 'My soul is overwhelmed with sorrow to the point of death' (Mark 14:34). It is a recognition that there is a part of us deep within.

5. You can't affect it directly

From the point of view of Christ's coaching of us, we cannot directly affect the soul ourselves. If the hidden central heating system breaks down it requires expert engineers to fix it – an employee with a spanner won't help. Only God can directly affect the soul. However, that doesn't mean that the work God accomplishes in our thinking, feelings and will, are irrelevant. Ideally we grow in our understanding of God and His Word. We think correctly, our negative and destructive feelings are replaced by better ones. Our will is released to act in love with the world around, and the body is freed to do the will of God with joy. But this takes seconds because the soul helps bring the aspects of our person together, enabling us to operate seamlessly as people. God works with us to do what we cannot do on our own.

6. God brings peace to our souls

In his chapter on the soul in *Renovation of the Heart*, Dallas Willard explains that the way of rest for our souls is to 'abandon outcomes'. Once we accept the yoke of Jesus' teaching, that we don't have it within ourselves to accomplish what we think we need, there is a great sense of peace. This is not the apathy of someone who 'can't be bothered to get their act together', just the quiet confidence that all is well because God has things in hand.

The way you live can nurture the life of God within you so that His streams of living water nourish you. Solitude and silence, looked at in the last chapter can help us. People can refresh our souls by the way they speak to us or write about God, or sing to us. We know that God is somehow touching the deepest part of us, through their activity.

WHAT JESUS DIDN'T SAY

Jesus doesn't focus on the soul as much as He does the rest of us. He knows that as believers grow in their walk with Christ, developing a trust in His life within them, and incorporating the practices of silence and solitude into their lives, they are bound to know a peaceful soul.

MAIN POINTS

- You have a soul that is constantly at work bringing together your thinking, feelings, choices and bodily reactions to make you who you are.
- Your soul is saved by Christ when you respond in faith to His call on your life.
- As we work with Christ in seeing the parts of our lives develop, so God works with our soul. So although we don't affect it directly, we can assist God in what He is doing with us.

ACTION

1. Plan to spend some time on your own reflecting on the pace of life. What could you do differently that would enable you to experience greater peace? Have you abandoned outcomes in the areas that are troubling you?
2. Have you neglected your soul? Ask God to bring to your soul the peace He promises.

Note

1. Dallas Willard, *Renovation of the Heart* (Navpress, 2002).

PART FOUR

Develop Team Spirit

The new kind of life is seen by how we relate to people. We were made for relationship, with God and others. Our rebellion against God has a knock-on effect; designed to move towards people, we invent our personal caves that we retreat to, or demand so much that people can't cope.

Much of Jesus' teaching shows us how we function with a new kind of life. God's love for us allows us to love others. We see this worked out in key aspects of our life as described in the Sermon on the Mount. The way we choose and manage words stands apart from the ways people generally try to operate. Lessons on community living are played out in the family and the church, yet Jesus' teaching stands against much modern practice. If we are living out this new kind of life, these environments will provide a great challenge.

Chapter 17

Love is easy if you know how

We might have expected that a meal in a restaurant in Disney World, Florida, was going to be unusual, but had we known it was going to be embarrassing, too, we would have eaten elsewhere. My wife and I thought it would be fun to eat in a fifties-themed restaurant, called the Prime Time Café. The 40-minute wait suggested the place was popular, and there were fifties films being shown on fifties-style US TVs to keep us occupied.

What we hadn't realised was that the waiters and waitresses had their own rather bizarre game. When our time to eat came we were summoned with the call, 'Cousin Pecks!' and taken to a table and told to 'introduce' ourselves to our 'cousins' who had 'popped over', who were no more than punters like us wondering what was going on. The waitress called herself Aunty and we were told to 'lay the table' and 'eat up or there would be trouble'.

Young and old were all treated with a patronising air, and homespun advice was issued when it was thought necessary. A teenage brother and sister were told by Aunty to be more pleasant to one another: 'If you don't get on now you will grow up to regret it and then it will be too late!'

In the world of Disney, everything is that easy. When rubbish is dropped it's instantly cleared away. When you find yourself peering at a map to find the way, a kindly Disney employee will appear from nowhere to help you (this happened to us three times) and there are no problems that can't be dealt with using a little 'Disney magic'. Apparently this extends to siblings getting on. Love is easy when you know how.

We have seen already how the Sermon on the Mount has some of the most challenging teachings in the whole of the New Testament. If we find the Law in the Old Testament impossible, then Jesus seems to make it worse. The level of relationship required is so high we imagine that only hermits could come close. And what of Jesus' command to love? What is He looking for from us? And how could we begin to do as He asks? Most of us don't live in Disney World.

The indicator

Superficial love is very easy. We can all fake a smile and gentle enquiry. But when Jesus asks us to love He means acting with good will towards others. Feelings are not absent, but biblical love has a strong action component. In fact Jesus makes our love a primary indicator of whether or not we truly love God. John would later say that we can't claim to love God whom we have not seen if we do not love those we have seen. Christians are to be known, not by their sound doctrine, zeal in evangelism or power of their miracles – but by their love for one another (John 13:34; 15:12,17). Jesus does not coach 12 isolated individuals one on one, but coaches them together so they can practise what He preached in community.

How do we do it?
1. Realise you are a lover

We were made for relationship. In relationship we reflect our Creator who as Father, Son and Holy Spirit lives in an eternal relationship of love. But relationships in a fallen world cause us pain. Instead of loving our 'neighbours' we withdraw from them, frightened that in giving of ourselves we may be rejected. Or we are concerned that we won't receive what we need from our relating and so we prefer to stay aloof rather than risk disappointment.

But the new kind of life changes all that. We know that God loves us warts and all. He fills the vacuum in our hearts that we thought we needed people to fill, and although we still need to be in community, our new life in Christ means that people, even a marriage partner, needn't bear the responsibility of making life work for us. God has taken care of this. This is how Jesus lived, in communion with His heavenly Father, and able to enjoy the friendship of the Twelve and others who supported Him, both men and women. So whatever you may believe about yourself, or have been told, or have sensed from others' reaction to you, you are a loving person deep down. You were made to love. The start to loving others is to realise who you are and that God's love for you can free you to love others.

2. Love God

In life love tends to be reciprocal. We have relationships that are give and take; you invite someone round for a meal, in due course they invite you back. You do a favour for a mate, they do one for you. No one's actually keeping score, but the fabric of civilised society depends on it.

So the command to love your enemies is tough. They elicit annoyance, anger and malice in us, not love. It is not only countercultural to love them, but seemingly impossible to do so with any degree of integrity. How can we love them? Do we fake it?

Look at Jesus' commands about love. Jesus said that if we were to concentrate on just one thing it would be to 'Love the Lord your God with all your heart and with all your soul and with all your strength and with all your mind"; and, "Love your neighbour as yourself."' (Luke 10:27). This love was a pivotal theme within Jesus' very last conversation with the Twelve, 'If you love me, you will obey what I command. And I will ask the Father, and he will give you another Counsellor to be with you for ever – the Spirit of Truth' (John 14:15–17).

In John 15 Jesus says that if the disciples remain 'in Christ' they will bear fruit (ie the qualities that God looks for). Later He says, 'As the Father has loved me, so have I loved you. Now remain in my love. If you obey my commands, you will remain in my love, just as I have obeyed my Father's commands and remain in his love' (15:9–10).

In these verses Jesus is saying that love is possible but only as we stay close to Him and obey Him. If we do, God will work with us enabling our growth. We learn something akin to the sort of fellowship Jesus also enjoyed with His Father. Love is easy when you know how.

Seeking to love someone without God's involvement, is like trying to speak another language without having first learnt it. No amount of effort is going to help. We can be dedicated, fervent, but nothing we say will be understood unless we are first taught what to say.

So, imagine for a moment someone who you struggle to love. How do you live this new kind of life? Jesus tells you to recall that God is your loving Father. He loves you and will provide for you in life. He cares for you and will never let you down, He has plans and purposes for you, He will daily sustain you. This is a simple but profound truth. If you don't know and feel the love of God yourself, it is hard to truly love others, for your relationships will be based on your deficit, not on God's bounty. A counsellor in a church we once attended had a saying: 'Hurt people hurt people', ie people who are hurt by others tend to choose to hurt others. But it is also true that 'loved people love people' – we seek the good of others when we know God's good will towards us. We can love them for God's sake.

Think now of the person you don't love. Why are you not able to seek their good? There could be a whole host of reasons, but each has an answer. Q. 'Do they not deserve it?' Answer, 'No, but then neither do you.' Q. 'Is there something repulsive in them?' Answer, 'That's not for you to judge and, anyway, prayer is more appropriate than "non-love".' As I recall God's love for me and His commitment to me I can say, 'OK I love others. I don't need to waste energy on myself; I don't need to judge them. I can be free to care for them.'

So, loving one another and serving one another becomes possible. We seek the good of the other person and are able to because we know that God's love is sufficient for us.

3. Love enemies

Jesus also says, 'But I tell you who hear me: Love your enemies, do good to those who hate you, bless those who curse you, pray for those who ill-treat you' (Luke 6:27–28a). How do you love someone who you know dislikes you and may not want you to live? Loving those who curse us takes this love further. When someone curses us, we respond to them with blessing, saddened that they should feel the need to be negative towards us and keen to put things right if the fault is with us.

We respond as those aware that we don't need to defend ourselves, or take offence. God is in control, He will vindicate us and if we are in the wrong we can happily put it right. Although they are hostile towards us, we are so blessed with the love of God that we can wish them well. As I hear Jesus' commands and am enabled to follow them, I become glad that He makes the standards so high. After all, if He let me get away with a hypocritical love that I somehow managed to summon up, I would be still battling away trying to 'be nice'. His higher demands force me to the Word and prayer to learn how. I don't have to be superficial; this is a new kind of life I am living.

WHAT JESUS DIDN'T SAY

The debased use of the love word means that we are often confused about what we need to do. We want to feel love before we give love and so end up doing very little. If love is seeking the good of others it is good practice to do it regardless. As we obey, we often find that our feelings will catch up with us. Remember that true love for someone is to show God's love, and this may not be comfortable for him or her. We don't measure whether we have loved by the person's response. The most loving thing may be to speak the truth in love, which can cause necessary short-term pain, but will be a true help in the long run.

MAIN POINTS:
- Christ coaches you to love others.
- Love is a vital sign that you have understood and grasped God's love for you.
- You cannot expect to love others without God's help, but with God's help, even love for enemies is possible.

ACTION

1. Ask God to help you to love those He brings across your path today.
2. If you struggle to love someone, start praying for him or her first. Ignore your feelings and ask God to bless him or her.
3. Make a list of the evidences of the love of God in your life. Thank Him!

Chapter 18

The new life works at all levels

The colleges I attended were wise in their interviewing procedure. Both Wye College, London University, and London School of Theology didn't just give me a formal interview with tutors, but also asked some students to show me round. Prospectuses paint one picture, tutors another, but it's the students that can tell you what it's really like. You can ask questions such as: 'How boring are the lectures?'; 'How little work can you get away with?'; 'Which courses should be avoided?' and 'Is the grant really enough?' (in the days when we had such things). It was in the interests of both the college and the student that I had the best possible understanding of whether this was the college for me.

Jesus wants us to understand what the new kind of life He promises is really like and how different it is from the way the world typically runs. We think we know what love looks like; we have experienced examples in our own life and maybe the church we are part of. But in case we are in any doubt, we have the Sermon on the Mount that represents Christ's charter for society. This is how you need to learn to love, He says. Don't be surprised, don't be confused. If you follow my kind of life – this is what is on the agenda.

So in order to further earth the teaching on love in the last chapter, we look at some passages from the Sermon on the Mount that explain how this works out in key relationships: with those close to us, those we come across and the person we marry. Remember these are not laws to obey as if failure leads to condemnation, but the sort of life followers of Christ are learning to live.

1. Taking care when you fly off the handle

'You have heard that it was said to the people long ago, "Do not murder, and anyone who murders will be subject to judgment." But I tell you that anyone who is angry with his brother will be subject to judgment.' (Matt. 5:21–22)

In the Sermon on the Mount, there is a logic in anger being one of the first areas that Jesus considers. In broad terms, anger comes when our will is crossed, which stems from a self-willed disposition. So our anger brings us face to face with the extent to which we have said goodbye to the old life when we joined with our Coach. If I am still harbouring desires to have my own way in life, then I will be angry often. This is largely a 'destructive' emotion, as we saw in Chapter 13, and will cripple our walk with Christ. Jesus' command does seem unreasonable, however. Why is my anger at 'my brother' subject to judgment as bad as if I had murdered him? The reason that anger is condemned is that so much else will accompany it. An angry emotion is one thing – the anger, our reaction to a crossed will, is not necessarily even a sin. But anger 'at my brother' involves a wilful act. If I choose to be angry at him, I can only do so if I believe I am justified in doing so, forgetting that I am a sinner too and err in ways that might provoke wrath in others. I can only retain anger if I emphasise my woundedness at his expense. I am thus embracing anger in a way that is inconsistent with one who tastes the love and mercy of God.

So whether or not I actually wish the person dead, my relationship with God is marred and needs to be sorted.

2. Be careful what you say

'Again, anyone who says to his brother "Raca," is answerable to the

Sanhedrin. But anyone who says, "You fool!" will be in danger of the fire of hell.' (Matt. 5:22)

Jesus moves on to explain how angry words are so destructive within community life. The word 'raca' was a term of contempt. We might say 'you idiot!' with a venom that implies that we don't think too much of them. In that day, society recognised the wrongness of such behaviour – the highest court in the land would punish anyone who spoke that way. The phrase, 'you fool' is, in the context, more serious. This intends greater harm, for it implies complete disdain for people. If 'you idiot' intends to hurt, 'you fool' cares little for them, whether they are hurt or not. They are disregarded, treated as dirt. This violated the soul and implied a complete disregard for the image of God within them.

Jesus is saying that such behaviour had no place at all in the kingdom. If we are loved by God and know His favour how can we treat others as if they don't matter?

3. Relationships above religion

'Therefore, if you are offering your gift at the altar and there remember that your brother has something against you, leave your gift there in front of the altar. First go and be reconciled to your brother; then come and offer your gift.' (Matt. 5:23–24)

In view of this attitude of love towards others, kingdom people are concerned to be at peace with anyone they meet or know. If they were giving a gift at the altar (a highly religious act) but realised that someone had something against them, it would be in their heart to sort it out, even if it wasn't their fault!

'Settle matters quickly with your adversary who is taking you to court. Do it while you are still with him on the way, or he may hand you over to the judge, and the judge may hand you over to the officer, and you may be thrown into prison. I tell you the truth, you will not get out until you have paid the last penny.' (Matt. 5:25–26)

The same is commanded of someone who is being sued. Your concern is to deal with the situation. Jesus knows that there will only be one winner (lawyers!) in any case, and it's likely to cost you. The phrase 'settle matters' implies an open-heartedness that is sad that the problem exists, and a concern that the suing party feels aggrieved. The disposition is: 'What can we do to help you'?

This command, coupled with the illustration about non-resistance in 5:38–42, have caused some to assume that Jesus is teaching that Christians should be doormats, especially when it comes to legal disputes. But they fail to realise that these examples are illustrations of the heart of the man or woman in the kingdom. It doesn't mean it is never appropriate to go to court, just that our disposition should be that we are more willing to settle in an amenable fashion. One charity allowed a situation to drag on for 20 years because of unwillingness to take a fellow Christian to court, despite his defiant response to reasonable requests. There will be some occasions when court action is the only action that is sensible and, if that's the case, we shouldn't feel that Jesus is condemning us.

4. Beware of your roving eye

'You have heard that it was said, "Do not commit adultery." But I tell you that anyone who looks at a woman lustfully has already committed adultery with her in his heart.' (Matt. 5:27)

If anger was an appropriate area to begin His teaching, it is no surprise that Jesus deals with sex soon after. Once again the teaching seems harsh. Avoiding adultery is in most people's power, but the prohibition on lusting seems at first sight to be impossible teaching. It's important to note that Jesus is not condemning sexual desire as such. It is a normal thing for us to find another attractive, and one reason why people decide to marry. There are some Christians who are convinced that God will want them to marry someone they don't fancy, but that says more about their view of God than it does about God's view of the matter. Jesus' concern is when a man or woman looks at someone intending to desire them sexually. Such behaviour treats the person purely as an object of sexual gratification and demeans them as a human being. So adultery may not have taken place, but the sin of the heart has been committed and is likely to bring discomfort to the party who is the object of desire, even if nothing is said and done. For many people this behaviour has become a habit. Any short-term benefit they may feel has unhelpful consequences, as the relationships with the opposite sex become strained and frustrating.

The cure for lust is love. If you are seeking the good of another, then however attractive you find him or her, you won't want to act on this attraction outside of a marital relationship, because you know to do this contravenes God's commands on the matter and won't be for his or her good. The occasion will always be an opportunity to go back to God that He may fill you with His love.

5. Smooth divorces are only in movies

'It has been said, "Anyone who divorces his wife must give her a certificate of divorce." But I tell you that anyone who divorces his wife, except for marital unfaithfulness, causes her to become an adulteress, and anyone who marries the divorced woman commits adultery.'
(Matt. 5:31–32)

Concern about anger, reconciliation and lust leads us logically to divorce. There was a dispute in Jesus' day over whether or not it was lawful to divorce on a whim. There were two 'houses' (schools of thought) among the Pharisees who were the learned and pious of the time. They were constantly opposed to each other and this included over divorce; Hillel said that various reasons could be given, including fancying another woman more than your wife; the school of Shammai insisted that only moral grounds qualified for divorce. With divorce becoming all too common, Jesus' words have been scrutinised today, not least because many want to know whether or not they are free to remarry if they have divorced.

Jesus anticipates the arguments but satisfies neither the legalists nor the libertines. He points out that divorce is never God's intent and leads to harm to both parties. This is not a 'lifestyle choice' but something that won't leave either person the same again. Jesus says that it is not enough for men to instigate divorce legally – there are heart issues involved. So, yes, divorce is permissible, but the reason given is not adultery – as if a marriage must end if adultery occurs – but the hardness of heart. Jesus says it is better for people to divorce rather than live in an intolerable situation and that adultery is not a necessary cause.

His comment about causing adultery needs to be understood carefully. In His day divorce meant the woman was left in a dreadful situation. There was no welfare state and a single woman had to hope that her family might help, or another man marry her. This is why Jesus says that divorcing without good reason (here marital unfaithfulness) leads her to 'remarry' and thus commit adultery.

Some Bible scholars argue that there are in total three reasons why someone might divorce and be permitted to remarry: abuse, adultery and abandonment (see also 1 Corinthians 7). The point of this passage is – don't leap into divorce, it's not God's ideal.

What Jesus didn't say

The commands of Jesus are often treated as case law, as if we are armed with a list of things to do or not do which we refer to as we go through the day. Jesus intends us to see the examples as describing the new kind of life we naturally lead as those who have confidence in Jesus. For those appropriately trained in the new life it becomes difficult to do the opposite. We feel wounded when we are angry at someone else, use contemptuous words or abuse our relationship with members of the opposite sex. The commands are necessary as a reminder, but if we naturally react angrily, the command is only of value to induce shame not to provide the will to do the opposite. Someone who works with God to produce the fruit of a renewed heart as we looked at earlier, will live the Sermon on the Mount almost without thinking.

Main points

- Jesus gives us examples of how the new kind of life is lived out.
- Knowing Jesus, affects our relationships with others; those who cross us, those we have disputes with, people we fancy and the person we are married to.

Action

1. Can you imagine yourself living the kind of life Jesus commands in this chapter?
2. Who could help you work out what you are truly like and pray with you towards your growth?

Chapter 19

If you deal in spin you are out of control

You are moving house. You desperately need your friends' help, but you know they don't get on with your sister. Do you tell them that the sister will be there?

Your children are desperate to go to the park. It has been a busy afternoon. You have guests coming and you are pretty sure you can't fit it in. But telling them that it might happen will buy you time. What do you say?

You hear that the minister has been given a raise in salary after a stormy leadership meeting where he apparently threatened to resign. But the person telling you isn't part of the church; they just know the minister's wife well. What do you do with the information?

Your aunt is coming around for a meal on Sunday. She hates religion. You know that *Songs of Praise* is on TV when she visits. Do you have the TV on in the hope that it gives you the opportunity to speak?

Your car has broken down and you need a car next day for work. Your friends have two cars, and you suspect one may not be used, but you don't want to put them in an awkward position. Do you phone them?

When Jesus describes the new kind of life to His followers, He is keen to impress upon them the importance of what they say. It is with our words that we influence others one way or another, building up or tearing down, informing or deceiving, communicating or ignoring. As James says in his letter, 'the tongue is a small part of the body, but it makes great boasts' (3:5). What we say is one of the most important things about us. If you were wired up for a whole day and your words were played to a friend, how would you feel?

What does Jesus say about our speech and how does He coach us to improve it?

1. Make it honest

'Simply let your "Yes" be "Yes", and your "No", "No"; anything beyond this comes from the evil one.' (Matt. 5:37)

It has become fairly common for some people to preface remarks in conversation, 'To be honest with you'. The speaker is rarely aware that what they are implying is that other parts of what they have said are lies! Many of the people I know who use the phrase wouldn't actually dream of deliberately lying, but this phrase and others such as: 'I swear to you,' 'Scout's honour', 'To be perfectly frank', are designed to help the hearer accept that the speaker is telling the truth. But they actually go further; they also aim to serve to impress the truth upon someone who may not naturally choose to believe it. Jesus says this attempt to manipulate behaviour is inconsistent with the people of God. We don't need to swear by anything – let your yes be yes and your no be no.

But why the explanation 'everything else is from the evil one'?

The devil is the 'father of lies' (John 8:44), so is always keen when we are tempted to lie. So Jesus is saying that any attempts to convince someone that we are telling the truth is the sort of thing the devil himself would do. The Christian should be known as being honest-speaking, not needing to embellish words, or make them sound important. We all know how politicians are rarely able to operate over any length of time if they have lied.

Kingdom people have nothing to hide and want others to be fully aware of what is going on. They would hate people to agree to something without the full facts being made available and would be horrified to think they felt as if they were kept in the dark.

This manipulation of the truth has become such a pattern of behaviour that some people don't even realise they are doing it. 'Will you help me, it will just take 10 minutes', they say, knowing it may take an hour. 'You will enjoy it', they say, knowing you are unlikely to. So, looking back to the beginning of this chapter, if you need help with your house and you know there may be friction, you really need to tell both parties. And if you know that you are unlikely to be able to take the children to the park, they need to know – they'll get over it!

2. Don't be judge and jury

'Do not judge, or you too will be judged. For in the same way as you judge others, you will be judged, and with the measure you use, it will be measured to you.' (Matt. 7:1–2)

Our capacity to have opinions and make assessments develops from a very young age. We have a good idea what's fair when we see the size of a sibling's bowl of ice cream, compared to ours. Some people never get beyond such rudimentary judgments; newspapers give column inches to adult versions of judgments that have moved little from the playground taunting of our youth.

Jesus isn't saying 'never judge', that would make fools of us all. We make judgment calls as we assess a whole manner of things in our daily lives as parents, workers and citizens. To judge means to estimate or prove, as when my dentist examines my teeth, or my employer considers the appointment of a colleague.

The judging Jesus condemns is the assessments we make as if we were God and had a right to condemn or blame another person or group of people. We assume that we have all the facts at our disposal, and are as impartial as God to make the call. Office gossip is not just fun and inquisitive but allows people to bolster their position in the 'pecking order' in an environment that is judge, jury and executioner. Jesus states it plainly: if we judge others, we will be judged ourselves. How often have we seen tit for tat squabbles played out within the home, the newspapers or the boardroom?

The person judged feels vulnerable immediately and promptly looks for weakness in the accuser. And of course they will be able to find it. Doing this shows we haven't truly grasped that kingdom righteousness is a gift. True understanding of God's mercy should stop us from feeling the need to make censorious judgments. We have admitted the worst things about ourselves, why do we need to judge others? So if you hear stories about the pastor's salary, it is not for you to make any judgment about it, or do anything at all. You haven't heard it first hand, and in any case the minister's salary is not your business. We have to bury any condemning disposition if we want to lift others out of sinful behaviour and only then if we have our facts straight and are keen to think and hope for the best in the person we want to help. Instead of condemning, the child of the King wants to bless others, praying that God may draw near and encourage them. We urge them to enter the kingdom where they can receive all they need for life in this world and the next.

3. Give truth when they are ready

'Do not give dogs what is sacred; do not throw your pearls to pigs. If you do, they may trample them under their feet, and then turn and tear you to pieces.' (Matt. 7:6)

Many have assumed that Jesus' command that you shouldn't throw pearls to swine must mean that Christians shouldn't keep communicating the gospel to people who clearly aren't interested, which is an attitude that flatly contravenes Jesus' earlier teaching! These critics even assume that they know who the swine are that they shouldn't speak with.

This approach is the opposite of the message of the new kind of life that Jesus freely offers to all. Jesus is actually speaking with tenderness about those who are outside the kingdom. The meaning of 'throwing pearls to swine' is that they are indigestible. Whatever the pearl quality they are no good to pigs. Indeed a hungry pig, fed up with such unpalatable grub, may well turn on the provider. Jesus is urging us to not force Christian truth on people who are not ready for it. We will not be thanked; we will only make them angry.

So you would probably be better off putting on a DVD of your aunt's favourite movie than forcing *Songs of Praise* on her.

4. Use requests to build relationships

> *'Ask and it will be given to you; seek and you will find; knock and the door will be opened to you. For everyone who asks receives; he who seeks finds; and to him who knocks, the door will be opened.'*
> (Matt. 7:7–8)

Any self-respecting male will tell you that you never ask for directions even when you know you are lost and any woman will laugh at what this odd quirk of behaviour says about the male ego. But it seems that the unwillingness to ask is rooted deep within the human personality. We prefer not to be in someone else's debt. Our self-sufficient outlook prevents us from appearing vulnerable. But Jesus encourages us to simply ask people for what we need.

Asking is a means of receiving God's benefits into our lives. These verses in Matthew 7 have often been used to apply to prayer, but from the context, I believe they could also apply to asking individuals. We should have the same attitude with people as we have with God. In simply asking people we build partnership and community and share together in enjoying life. So if you need a car for work at short notice, ask. Give your friends plenty of opportunity to say no, maybe ask their advice. There may be another solution.

There's a contrast between asking and demanding. When we demand we put the person on the back foot and are likely to create a reaction we don't want. People who would have granted a simple request feel violated when we demand something, because they feel we are trying to take away their choice. A demand implies that we fear they wouldn't willingly give what we want and so we have to put the pressure on.

This manipulative bullying has become a normal procedure for some, both within the home where parents effectively bully their children to behave in certain ways, and at work where managers use their power to force employees to work as they want. But the transformation that occurs in our relationships when we simply ask can be very fast. Jesus clearly implies that the procedure of 'ask, seek, knock' can be one that 'works' as we interact with others and will lead us on into the right attitude to God when we pray (see Chapter 10).

What Jesus didn't say

The sins of speech are as big a problem as any within the Church. Here's why. We live in a physical world and yet believe and accept a view of reality that is not seen. We live a natural and also a supernatural life. We look for God to do things, which we don't yet experience. So there are plenty of opportunities for us to say that things are different from what they really are. We can put a spiritual spin on things that is not warranted by God or His Word, in an attempt to comfort ourselves that the new kind of life is one that we are living. Humility is required as we stick to the truth, acknowledge failure and rejoice in success and look to God so that when He works we won't need hype to express it – it will be clear for all to see.

Main points
- Our Coach is looking for you to use speech wisely: being honest, non-judgmental, sensitive in witness and clear in what you want.
- Many Christians have fallen into habits of speech that are not in keeping with the new kind of life.

Actions
1. Our speech is an overflow of the life of God within us. At the end of a day, reflect on what you can remember about what you have said and the way you have said it. Ask your Coach to reveal to you what this says about your heart.
2. Revisit this at the end of every week and ask Jesus to help you make progress.

Chapter 20

Jesus isn't comfortable at some churches

You move to a new area, or you have just become interested in Christianity. You know the best place to learn from Christ is likely to be in a community of believers. Your growth depends to some extent on the wise counsel of other Christ-followers who provide models of how you can live in the twenty-first century and provide opportunities to live out the new kind of life with people around you. But when it comes to deciding which particular community of believers to join, you are 'spoilt for choice'. What does Jesus say about the church community?

1. Keeping the main thing the main thing

Most people think of church as an old building with stained-glass windows and a spire or tower, where regular services, weddings and funerals take place. But we could search the Gospels for a long time before we find any mention of teaching on much of what we associate with church. Jesus saved a wedding, providing some exquisite wine when the hosts faced the total embarrassment of running out, and stopped a funeral in its tracks to raise the young man who had died. But two incidents of this nature is hardly advice on good practice for the modern cleric.

Jesus said that He would build His Church 'and the gates of Hades will not overcome it' (Matt. 16:18), but there's no specific advice on the style of the meeting place, the style of service, the optimum length of services, the number of services or the specific content of those services. This is in part because His ministry anticipates the church communities that would gather following His ascension and the coming of the Spirit, as people responded to the message of the new kind of life and met to learn together how this works out in practice. The detail of the gatherings is left to the community of believers in their culture and situation. He is less concerned about service style and architecture than He is about building community around the Word of God. His community of 12, and the larger groups that He also taught, were small prototypes of what church is like.

For Jesus, you can be sure that His concern is that the Great Commandment (love one another – John 13:34) and the Great Commission (make disciples – Matt. 28:19–20) are practised. Whatever else happens, gather and teach believers, that their corporate life might demonstrate the reality of the new kind of life they share.

Thus our first concern in finding a church, or seeking to influence churches we are part of, is that some focus is given to these two dimensions:

- *Is it a loving company of people focused on God's Word?*
- *Is it looking to communicate the good news of Christ's new kind of life to the community in which it's placed and beyond?*

If it is, it's in harmony with Christ, whatever else it does or does not do.

In my opinion, it is worth travelling a reasonable distance to be part of a community that keeps the main thing the main thing, providing we can function sensibly within that community – a Sunday commute that is so far away that there is no chance of any other contact during the week simply won't work. You will want to be involved with a smaller group of believers who can really get to know you, and you them.

The focus on these priorities will help us when it comes to areas where Christians in good conscience disagree. For example,

Christians disagree about when we should be baptised: as an infant as a sign by the parents of their willingness to bring us into the covenant relationship with God that they enjoy, or when we have come to faith and can make our own decision to follow Christ? I believe in the latter, but understand those that in good conscience hold to the former. Either way it's most important that the church teaches our utter dependence upon God's work in our daily lives and walk. Whether baptised as an infant or a believer, are we currently 'baptised' (immersed) in the Spirit of God? Churches have argued vehemently that they are correct about the mode of baptism, but seem to have missed the essential point!

Similarly, Christians have differing interpretations and language for the Communion service. The only explicit service direction Jesus gives is recorded by Luke (and outside the Gospels by Paul in 1 Corinthians 11) who tells us that the Passover meal, recorded also in Matthew and Mark, is to be changed and given a new meaning in remembrance of Him. But the frequency is left open and Jesus would no doubt be bemused and dismayed at some of the theological argument that has surrounded this essentially simple remembrance service.

It is not my intention to explain the differing interpretations, and I am not pretending that they aren't of great significance. My point here is to underline that whatever the church believes, it should stress the vital importance of acknowledging our dependence on Christ's death and resurrection as we share in the benefits of the new covenant.

Chances are you won't find the ideal church in every respect, but if you look for ones that keep the main thing the main thing, you won't go far wrong.

2. Freedom to serve

If it's crucial that the Great Commandment and the Great Commission are practised, it is also important that you be encouraged to play your part. At one level, no one can stop you, but it makes things a good deal easier if the community that you are part of encourages you to serve in the ways your Coach is directing. Aside from assigning

Peter a key role of helping build the Church (Matt. 16:18), fulfilled by his Pentecostal sermon and Early Church leadership, Jesus is clear that He expects all His followers to be involved in communicating the gospel. The provision of a main man (or woman in some cases) as the paid servant of the people can serve to assist this process. Many churches would disintegrate overnight without the unstinting service of believers set aside to lead. But too often the 'minister becomes the focal point'. The mentality that 'we pay you to do the work' damages the process entirely and makes low assumptions of the members. Perhaps this is why Jesus specifically says we should not give people titles. He uses the examples of Father, and teacher. Would Jesus have supported the title Reverend? Or any other church officer? Maybe He doesn't mind, but if the title serves to create an inappropriate gap between the members of the church and the leadership, or inappropriate expectations of the leader, then it is doing more harm than good. We will see in Chapters 21 and 22 that we all have a role to play.

In most churches the leadership play a crucial role in the way the community operates. So we do well to ask whether the leadership enables or stifles the work of God's Spirit within those that gather? In Mark 10, Jesus rebukes James and John for assuming a domineering style of leadership rather than one that is service based (10:43–45). The rest of the New Testament is clear that biblical leadership has a strong serving component. Our Coach is looking for you to work with Him in seeing great things happen. It is a significant help if your church leaders share that desire.

3. Mixing in the community

We are taught to love everyone, even our enemies, that the world will hate the believer as it hated Jesus and that persecution is likely. But Jesus does not warn us about being 'contaminated by the world'. Why?

Jesus focuses on the heart, not on the outward temptations we face. In Mark 7:20, He says that it is from within that evil comes. I can't be contaminated by things outside me. If I am tempted by something or someone it makes sense to stay away from it, but the problem for me is within my heart, not in the thing itself. Jesus isn't condoning the sort of places that Christians would regard as unhealthy today, He is merely saying that Christians are far more concerned about their life before God than they are with being condemnatory. There are no lists of areas to avoid, but rather attitudes to cultivate.

Jesus sees the whole of life to be lived for God, not with the sacred/secular divide that mars many Christians' outlook, where 'the sacred' – church, Bible, prayer time, meeting with Christians – is set against 'the secular' – work, leisure, going out, entertainment. Jesus' life has one label – all of life was to be lived within the kingdom of God. You are no less Christian in taking a board meeting than a prayer meeting, though I have a friend who forgot where he was and came close to opening in prayer at work. You play the violin as a Christian, sell cars as a Christian, and raise children as a Christian. You may not receive the help you think you need from the local church but still whatever you do can be for the glory of God. Jesus spent the bulk of His life working as a carpenter and His deity was not diminished one bit.

So don't be fooled when church notices, notice sheets and conversations focus on what takes place in the church building. This is not more important, though shouldn't be dismissed. Your work/home life is also part of what God is concerned with and He notices even if the notice sheet never does.

4. A church for the family?

Despite the way many churches are structured, 'family' seems to represent a low priority for Jesus. He wants churches to be like a family, but the few references to the nuclear family are reminders that they shouldn't obstruct what God is seeking to do in our lives. When Jesus was told that His own family was looking for Him, He seems almost dismissive: 'My mother and brothers are those who hear God's word and put it into practice' (Luke 8:21). He also warns that allegiance to Him is likely to split families: 'Brother will betray brother to death, and a father his child. Children will rebel against their parents and have them put to death. All men will hate you because of me, but he who stands firm to the end will be saved' (Mark 13:12–13).

'Do you think I came to bring peace on earth? No, I tell you, but division. From now on there will be five in one family divided against each other, three against two and two against three. They will be divided, father against son and son against father, mother against daughter and daughter against mother, mother-in-law against daughter-in-law and daughter-in-law against mother-in-law.' (Luke 12:51–53)

Jesus is not unconcerned about His own family. Luke tells us that He was obedient to His parents and, at the time of the cross, He passes His mother to John's trust – hardly the actions of a man indifferent. But He doesn't make the family any more important than it needs to be. Whether we are part of a large family unit including children and grandparents, or the classic family unit of 2.4 children, we are reminded that family must not become an idol.

Jesus gives no advice on how to bring up children, understand adolescent behaviour or care for the elderly. We must not interpret the silence as indifference, rather that for Jesus, all the teaching He gives about our human relationships applies equally to the family unit. Family is not a parallel universe where the decencies and assumptions of normal life don't apply. Parents bully children unaware that they may be partly to blame for the anti-social behaviour they see in them. They force their own Christianity upon them in a manner that Jesus spoke against when He warned about feeding pearls to swine (the lesson being, give people truth when they are ready to digest it). Conversely, children treat parents as people they can manipulate to get their ends, despite knowing that such treatment of their peers would be given short shrift. When they grow older, they contribute to the parent's loss of dignity by making unilateral decisions for their apparent good but ultimately to make life easy for themselves.

So when Jesus speaks of a new kind of life and loving those around us, the family unit is to be a key arena for this to be worked out. Everything said about loving others is to be true for the family. Being married to somebody, or being the natural parent of somebody, doesn't give us the right to treat him or her like a nobody. So, of course, you will be concerned that your family be catered for in the church you choose, but make sure that you are not expecting the church to do for your family what you should be doing.

What Jesus didn't say

We have noted that Jesus made no mention of service content, service length, style of music, size of church, building or style of building, 'ministers', spiritual gifts, leadership structure. The rest of the New Testament gives us instruction on some of these, but Jesus' priorities surround the living and sharing of the new kind of life in the world. If this isn't happening, church is a dangerous distraction, and Jesus wouldn't feel comfortable there, whatever else goes on.

Main points

- When deciding which church community to be part of, try those where the command to love one another, and to share the new kind of life are given priority.
- Look for a church where the leaders encourage you to serve.
- An over-emphasis upon church buildings and titles can work against the growth of the kingdom.
- All of life is to be for God – there's no sacred–secular divide.
- The new kind of life needs to apply to the family unit as much as to the rest of our relationships.

Action

1. Try and use the language the way Jesus and the New Testament used it. Don't think of church as the building, or certain meetings as 'worship' or certain people as 'special'. Church is people, all of life is worship and everyone is special, and every Christian has a 'special ministry' (though they may not have discovered it yet). Using language biblically will be a struggle because everyone around you will be locked into the same paradigm.
2. Ask gentle questions to help others see what Jesus intended and pray that things will increasingly be what He would want, in you, your family and church community.
3. Ask your Coach how He wants you to serve and look for opportunity, inside and outside the church community

PART FIVE

Work on His wavelength

Because Christianity has become divorced from discipleship, Christians see their service for God as an optional extra. In fact it is the heartbeat of the new kind of life. From day one the Twelve were part of the Jesus team which was making the kingdom available to others. The new kind of life was for sharing. It is an adventure that will leave you spoilt for everything else. Your involvement in sharing this life and blessing others will define who you are.

This means you are part of a spiritual battle and will face persecution and tough times. But this serves only to increase your sense that this life is the one for you. You find that your resources become His resources, a joy to have and use, and a joy to give away. After all, when you have His treasure, why would you need to worry about anything else?

Chapter 21

Christ offers adventure

Think back to your youth and you can probably remember a TV programme that got your pulse racing. For me there were more than a few – a sure sign of a misspent youth. *Mission Impossible* was one of the first, a sixties show now given modern popularity by the *Mission Impossible* films starring Tom Cruise. Maybe it was the formula I liked: Jim Phelps would be summoned to a location and directed to a tape recorder which would inform him of an international problem that needed sorting. His final instruction would begin, 'Your mission Jim, if you decide to accept is ...' And of course Jim always did accept before the recorder delivering the message promptly self-destructed. The programme had everything; mystery, danger, a mission that mattered and baddies overturned – which all appealed to my eight-year-old mind, and still seems quite fun a few decades later.

One of the saddest aspects of the malaise into which some forms of Christianity have fallen is that there is so little sense of adventure. God has built us for 'mission impossible' feats, but we settle for play school.

Yet when the first disciples were called they were immediately engaged in the mission of Jesus. Peter, Andrew, James and John were told that Jesus would make them 'fishers of men' (Matt. 4:19–22). The metaphor, taken from their own profession, also picked upon the Old Testament picture of God gathering people who would escape His judgment. Matthew is called from his tax-collecting booth (Mark 2:14) and immediately throws a party for his colleagues and friends to tell them who Jesus is (2:15). This new kind of life was to be communicated to everyone, and Jesus was building a team to do so. Look at His instruction when He calls them.

> 'He called his twelve disciples to him and gave them authority to drive out evil spirits and to heal every disease and sickness' (Matt. 10:1).
>
> 'As you go, preach this message: "The kingdom of heaven is near"' (Matt 10:7).
>
> 'Calling the Twelve to him, he sent them out two by two and gave them authority over evil spirits' (Mark 6:7).
>
> 'When Jesus had called the Twelve together, he gave them power and authority to drive out all demons and to cure diseases, and he sent them out to preach the kingdom of God and to heal the sick' (Luke 9:1–2).
>
> 'After this the Lord appointed seventy-two others and sent them two by two ahead of him to every town and place where he was about to go' (Luke 10:1).

On one occasion Jesus urged someone not part of the Twelve or 70 to follow Him in preaching the kingdom of God (Luke 9:60).

With authority

They were to share in the activity of Jesus. The word apostle means 'sent one' – one with the authority of the one sending. The apostles were given the power by God to announce the coming kingdom. They had entered into the kingdom (a new kind of life) and it was their task to welcome others to be part of the new community that Jesus was setting up and which would expand in a worldwide revolution as people were added from every ethnic background.

Yet novices

We might expect fast-track learning for the Twelve, but it seems the disciples were given the task of declaring the kingdom of God's nearness before they had understood a great deal of the precise nature of Jesus' ministry. As Jews they would have been familiar with the Old Testament, so they would have a foundational knowledge of God but it is clear that they were still learning who Jesus was as they told what they knew about the new kind of life. There is no evidence that they had made much progress in character development though doubtless itinerant lifestyle gave much opportunity for impromptu conversations. But as far as Jesus was concerned they didn't need to know very much. They had seen the demonstration of the kingdom and acted rather like bystanders summoned by news reporters to tell what they had just seen.

The entrustment of novices with the task of healing the sick and casting out demons sounds remarkable. After all there are special priests in some denominations set aside for this activity and in the wider Church there are those who have specialised ministries in this area. But as far as Jesus was concerned this was the normal practice for disciples called to serve with Him. They went with His authority.

Us and them

As we try and understand how Christ coaches us, we need to decide whether the mandate that Jesus gave the apostles is identical to that which He gives us. Did the apostles teach that preaching, healing and casting out demons was to be the normal pattern for all believers in Christ?

The answer is, 'yes and no'. The Early Church encouraged all people to be witnesses of the reality of Christ in their lives, though it seems that some had a distinct ministry in evangelism (Eph. 4:11). We are all free to pray for healing (Eph. 6:18), though some have special healing gifts (1 Cor. 12:9) and those who are sick are encouraged to call the elders in a local congregation to pray for them (James 5:14). The practice of casting out demons is not a focus of the New Testament letters, though the authority of believers over demons is clear (James 4:7) and the New Testament writers acknowledge the presence and power of the demonic (1 Cor. 12:10; 2 Cor. 10:3–6; Eph. 6:12).

As disciples of Jesus, we too are called to be 'fishers of men', making disciples as Jesus commands in Matthew 28:18–20. Not all will have the God-given ability to see God heal people on a regular basis, but we are all free to pray for the sick. Every church should be prepared, or know someone who is prepared, to cast out demons as and when they are manifest.

Your ministry

But whether or not you are gifted in the ways the apostles were, Jesus is coaching you to see yourself as His minister. This may sound strange and you may not be comfortable with the title or feel 'worthy'; you may not even like the responsibility. But as a Christ-follower you have no option. Too often Christians have sidestepped what should be their true calling by assuming they are part of the 'laity' and giving titles to those trained for particular roles. This permeates church life and in some cases the 'paid ministers' are not keen to acknowledge that their fellow believers have a 'ministry'. But don't be put off. Jesus calls the shots and He has things for you to do. Your development will typically take place in a local church where more experienced believers can give guidance and feedback to guide your ministry in ways that enhance the work of the church. But it is a mistake to limit your thinking to the local church or to expect that they will always be equipped and able to develop you as Jesus would.

God has placed you where He can use you. You are already a witness (whether you like it or not). Your network of friends and family, work colleagues and leisure contacts are the people God sends you to minister to. You don't need qualifications from a college, or a religious title in front of your name. God's intention is that everyone He calls should serve Him in sharing the new kind of life with others. If we really grasped the exciting possibilities of working with God to see people get to know Him, we would be dying to get even more involved. The Spirit within us is centrifugal – always pushing us out to share the good news of knowing God. This is mission that's possible and an adventure to which God calls us all. Will you decide to accept?

What Jesus didn't say

Jesus didn't say we would be judged on how many friends, family, or contacts, come to faith as a result of our work. If people are running away as soon as you try to engage in conversation with them, you would be wise to consider your approach, but the process whereby someone comes to faith is too complex to analyse. You may have a role in someone's conversion as part of a chain of events that you know nothing about or be involved in someone's conversion without any prior involvement. Our job is to share God's love and life wherever we can. We leave the results to Him.

Main points

- Life as a Christian can be an adventure.
- We are all called to communicate the new kind of life with those we know.
- Your 'ministry' is similar to the apostles that Jesus coached, so don't be put off – see yourself as someone who is engaged in Christ's mission.

Actions

1. See yourself as a minister. You may have only just got used to the name Christian, so minister seems like rapid promotion! You need to work on your self-talk. Jesus is telling you that this is who you are and He intends to work with you to produce fruit. Exciting eh?
2. What would be your mission possible? Ask the Coach what He thinks, and do something about it.

Chapter 22

Being a Christian is a big enough job for anyone

The church I grew up in on the Isle of Wight did not have a 'paid minister', preferring to make use of the gifts of its members (who are of course ministers), and 'visiting speakers' to lead and preach at services. I don't recall his name, but one visiting preacher reminded us forcibly that the church was there to reach out to 'non Christians' and that personal witness was a necessary part of every believer's life. As a young believer who preferred to keep quiet about my faith, I took this to heart and can recall the sense of guilt that I felt. On the Monday morning after this 'encouragement' I determined to do my bit when I went to school. I mustered the courage to tell a friend that I had been to church the day before, the best thing I could think of that would enable me to 'speak for Jesus' and appease the guilt. I felt very awkward doing it and to my knowledge it had no positive effect. I stayed quiet until made to feel guilty again.

Looking back I have no doubt that the preacher meant well, and of course personal witness is a crucial part of any believer's life, but I was never taught how to go about it. Any anecdotes from the pulpit seemed a mile away from what I was prepared to do. Indeed I was well into my later teens before I was able to be relaxed about talking about my faith. But Jesus calls us to be 'fishers of men' as we saw in the last chapter. Even if we aren't gifted evangelists, we still need to be prepared speak about our faith. Some we will create, some will fall into our lap. How should we go about it?

1. Live as a messenger of God

We noted in the last chapter that Christians are called into an adventure with God that beats any pursuit that they might choose to engage in. They find that the influence they wield within their home or work life is nothing compared to being involved with God in changing people's lives for good.

A quick run through some of the mentions of the Word of God in the Gospels reminds us that it is a potent force.

> 'Blessed rather are those who hear the word of God and obey it' (Luke 11:28).
> 'He told them, "This is what is written: The Christ will suffer and rise from the dead on the third day, and repentance and forgiveness of sins will be preached in his name to all nations ..."' (Luke 24:46–47).
> 'The words I have spoken to you are spirit and they are life' (John 6:63).
> 'You will know the truth, and the truth will set you free' (John 8:32).

A word from us can literally stop someone in their tracks and turn them around and start the new life that Jesus offers. Jesus tells us that the Holy Spirit is at work convicting the world of sin, righteousness and judgment – in other words He works on the inside as we work on the outside! He ensures that our words penetrate more deeply than the surface, creating real awareness that there's something to respond to.

But I need to add that the Word of God is not magic. Speaking in 'the name of Jesus' does not mean we get the results we want, like a magician. It is not automatic for people to respond affirmatively when they hear the Word (note the parable of the sower in Luke 8:1–15), but with that important rider understood, it should also be noted that it is God's normal means of working in someone's life.

2. Make good news the basis of your talk about God

Some Christians spend longer telling their friends and family what will happen if they don't believe the good news than what will happen if they do. And let's face it, many friends of Christians know the patter and aren't impressed. God can use the crassest techniques, but this was not the way our Coach operated. The vision of the kingdom should be the dominant feature of the message – we offer people a new kind of life, good news in this life and the next. We tell them that God is working in our world and they can be a part of it. Bad news must be mentioned, and it formed part of Jesus' message, but not in the finger-pointing 'scare you into the kingdom' sense.

You will need to think carefully before you speak; after all, Jesus and His disciples spoke to people who knew the Old Testament Law and had an expectation of a kingdom to come after death. There were hooks upon which Jesus and the apostles could hang the message. Our listeners may be less well informed; I once gave a hitchhiker a lift up the M3 who, on hearing that I was a minister, started asking about Moses' role as one of the apostles ... So we will need to assess the understanding of our audience before explaining the good news of the kingdom, which may mean asking questions before we launch into material that will be misunderstood. We live this side of the cross, and like the apostles post-resurrection, need to include explanation of how the death and resurrection of Christ are crucial events for God's work in our lives today. The apostle Paul said he 'preached Christ crucified'. The one who is King was also the suffering servant whose death on our behalf and in our place allowed God's anger against sin to be satisfied and enables forgiveness and new life. If we leave out the cross we have only delivered part of the message.

3. Ask good questions

In his book *How to Win Friends and Influence People*, Dale Carnegie said that good conversationalists listen for twice as long as they speak. It's not a bad principle to adopt when communicating the faith. It can be tempting to assume that communicating to others means us doing the talking, but too often our words fail to persuade because we haven't taken the time to get to know the person or understand what they need to hear. For this reason the art of asking good questions is vital. It was learning this skill that took a lot of the fear out of my faltering attempts at personal witness. There was none better than Jesus, a Man who knew the answers.

For example: 'What do you think, Simon?' (Matt. 17:25). 'What do you think?' (Matt 18:12); 'What do you think?' (Matt 21:28); 'What do you think about the Christ?' (Matt 22:42); 'Which of these three do you think was a neighbour?' (Luke 10:36). On more than one occasion we read that Jesus knew what someone was thinking. He knew what was in men's hearts (eg Mark 2:8). But we mustn't assume this was a manipulative device. Jesus was genuinely interested in engaging with people.

So what sort of questions might we ask? Here are a few suggestions:

- Have you ever had a religious experience?
- What do you think happens when we die?
- What do you think about church?
- If you could know God personally, would you want to?
- If there were a God what sort of a God would you like Him to be?

Some people have found their ability to talk to people about their faith transformed by being prepared to ask questions. What do you think?

4. Be single minded
The announcement of the coming kingdom was deemed the most important task for the followers of Jesus. They saw how Jesus even passed up an opportunity for a healing surgery in order to move on to the next village (Mark 1:21).

During one feedback session, the disciples became especially excited that they had seen demons expelled (Luke 10:17). Most believers would doubtless react the same. However, Jesus' response is that they should rejoice that their names are written in heaven.

The focus of Jesus' ministry was the message, not the manifestation of God's power. God may intervene in a person's life in healing or some other visible way, but this was not to be the focal point of the apostles' work. It is the miracle of new birth that we must pray for.

If we take this priority of Jesus seriously it will transform the way we understand our lives. We see our job as something we do along with Jesus, who teaches us how to do the job in the way He would do it if He were us. Too often we talk of ourselves in terms of our job.

'What do you do?'

'I'm a school teacher.'

But it is a small step from answering the question that way, to actually seeing our identity as a schoolteacher: this is why I go to work, this is what I am paid to do. Being a Christian should be the noun. I know a doctor who says: 'I am a Christian who happens to be a doctor.' In other words, his primary calling is as a disciple of Jesus, focused on fishing for men and women – his arena of life and influence is as a doctor. He still works hard as a doctor, and justifies his salary, but he knows that God is his ultimate employer (Col. 3:23–24).

5. Be prepared for the unexpected

When you examine the ministry of Jesus you find a mixture of planning and spontaneity. He visited the villages and towns in the area and knew His long-term goal was to head for Jerusalem. Luke makes this a key part of his Gospel. Some see his statement of Jesus' intent a pivotal part of the Gospel. 'As the time approached for him to be taken up to heaven, Jesus resolutely set out for Jerusalem' (Luke 9:51). But most of His individual confrontations came when people approached Him. In John's Gospel He was met by Nicodemus, the woman at well, the man at the pool. The woman caught in adultery is brought to Jesus (John 8:3). In Mark 2, His sermon is interrupted by four men lowering their friend through the roof, and Jairus asks Jesus to heal his daughter. On the way to meet her, He is touched by a woman with an ongoing menstrual problem.

You and I won't have the ministry Jesus had, but this model is a useful one to note. It seems the work of helping others recognise that there is a new kind of life is a mixture of planned events and ad hoc events. For you this may mean signing up to teach the Sunday school, or youth group, or a regular visit to a nursing home. But in your routine you still need to be open to chat with the office cleaner, the fellow boardroom director or the taxi driver. It is unlikely that we will be approached by the kind of people who met Jesus, but it's amazing how often I find that God gives me opportunities in conversation when I ask Him, and how much time goes by with no conversations of gospel significance when I don't.

6. Tell stories

One of the most fascinating parts of Jesus' communication was His use of stories. It was so prevalent that Gospel writers say that 'he did not say anything to them without using a parable' (Matt. 13:34). Stories raise interest levels. As a lay preacher I can see people engage more easily with what I am saying when I tell a story to illustrate a point. But in the case of Jesus, stories had an ability to give a sting in the tale (pun intended). People listening would discover that Jesus was directing His words at them. Stories are a great device for piercing our defence mechanisms. We find the story of the two sons (also known as the story of the Prodigal Son) is told when Jesus was criticised for spending time with people who the religious leaders thought were undesirable – the tax collectors and sinners. So Jesus tells a story about a father's lavish acceptance of his son who had engaged in all manner of undesirable activities, and the anger of the other son who had remained outwardly loyal but was inwardly antagonistic and hard-hearted towards his own brother. It wasn't hard for the religious leaders to realise who Jesus was getting at.

However, in spite of the easiness of the stories, Jesus' motive was not necessarily clarity. Jesus tells stories so that those who are really interested in the kingdom can benefit and those whose hearts are hardened can be confirmed in their prejudice (Matt. 13:13–15).

How are you intending to speak about your faith? Do you have a personal story to tell? It can be a great way in, providing your experience is not all you focus on. Sometimes giving a copy of biography and testimony can help people grasp the reality of the gospel before they delve into the Bible for themselves.

7. Expect signs following

The disciples saw significant things happen when they spoke of the good news (Matt. 10:7). The reactions were varied, as we have already noted, but there was a reaction. The ministry of the Twelve was unique; we needn't expect to have to shake the dust off our feet (Matt. 10:14) and few of us will depend on hospitality for our food and shelter. Nevertheless we should expect God to work. His power is available, the powers of darkness are real and so our obedient focus on God and His purposes will have an impact, in tangible obvious ways and within the inner lives of people we speak with. Sometimes it will take time. There are believers who have been faithful in sharing their faith to individuals for many years, without apparent fruit. Some missionaries have very few converts to show for a lifetime's endeavour. But God is at work and ultimately their work will be vindicated, even if they don't see it in their lifetime.

WHAT JESUS DIDN'T SAY

Stories abound of successful personal witness, and it is tempting to want to bottle the success and pour it out ourselves. But we have to find our way of sharing our faith in the context of our own personality, background and interests. There are types of people that only you can reach, so don't try and be someone you are not, using techniques and approaches that aren't natural to you. On the other hand don't be surprised if God uses you out of your comfort zone. He often does.

MAIN POINTS
- Christ is teaching you to communicate the new kind of life with others.
- You need to see yourself as a Christian before anything else.
- Communicate wisely, using questions, telling stories and focusing on good news.
- God will give you success in His time and His way.

ACTION

1. If you find the whole business of telling someone about your faith awkward, tell them. You might as well be honest, and it can save you unnecessary embarrassment.
2. Ask God for opportunities to speak about some aspect of your faith in the next week.

Chapter 23

The devil is defeated

There are people who like playing games and people who like to win. Those who like playing games have the motto, 'it's not the winning, it's the taking part'. Those who play to win have the motto, 'There are no prizes for being second'. Whether you are competitive or not, figuring out the purpose of the game is pretty crucial. There's a saying in golf, 'It's not how, but how many.' The aim of the game when all is said and done is to get the ball in the hole in the fewest strokes possible – the quality of your swing is irrelevant. Football is about scoring more goals than the opposition. How many fans have seen a team putting on more pressure, forcing more corners, yet ending up losing?

The sporting metaphors to describe the Christian life can be very clichéd. But when it comes to the subject of spiritual warfare, the competitive aspect is very strong: the very opening to Christ's ministry – 40 days in the wilderness tempted by the devil – sets the scene for the conflict and ultimate outcome. His friend John would later say that the 'reason the Son of God appeared was to destroy the devil's work' (1 John 3:8). The aim of the game for Christ was pretty clear and He wasn't playing for fun: *free people from captivity and render the enemy a fatal blow.*

He wants us to be in no doubt of the nature of the battle we have joined and what the tactics are for ensuring that we share in His victory.

1. The opposition

It is clear from Jesus' description that the devil has power. He describes him as 'the tempter' (Mark 4:1) and 'the prince of this world' (John 12:31). This is the one who snatches the Word of God away from people (Mark 4:15), is able to affect Peter's thoughts (Luke 22:31) and influence the Jews against Jesus (John 8:44). It is Satan who 'enters Judas' (John 13:27) who goes on to betray Jesus.

Furthermore, as a fallen angel he has power over other spirits who can have influence in the lives of people. In Mark's Gospel a man with an evil spirit confronts Jesus (1:24); a man is so overcome with evil spirits that no one could help him (5:2ff); and we read of a lad who from childhood had been possessed by an evil spirit (9:17). When the Gospel writers describe Jesus healing crowds of people, they invariably describe people with 'evil spirits' (Matt. 4:24). No one who reads the Gospels is left in any doubt that Satan and the evil spirits are active in the nation.

2. Christ's victory

Read the Gospels and you find Satan and his work is always described in the context of Christ's ultimate victory over him. When I was a student I was involved in planning the Christian Union's teaching programme. We had a policy of trying to cover all major doctrines within three years and the title of the talk would be written on a large blackboard for everyone in the college to see. We had a dilemma when it came to the devil. How could we convey the title without making it seem we had a fascination with him? 'Who is Satan?' hardly seemed appropriate, though it conveyed what we wanted to know. In the end we chose to call it, 'The Devil Defeated'.

The defeat of the devil is hinted at in Jesus' first confrontation in Matthew 4 where we read that Jesus is led by the Spirit into the desert to be tempted by the devil. This is not a heavyweight boxer running scared of his major contender and ending up being forced to fight for the world crown – the Spirit orchestrates this. Satan tempts Jesus to perform a miracle to feed His physical needs, to demonstrate His spiritual ability and obtain worldwide domination. Each time,

He replies with the Word of God. He lives according to a different reality than Satan and doesn't falter. The rest of the Gospels would emphasise His crucial victory over temptation in those 40 days.

His victory over Satan is reinforced in the rest of the Gospels. In Matthew 12 Jesus says that the victory over demonic forces is a sign that His kingdom is come (v.28). In Luke 11:22 He likens himself to a strong man who overcomes a burglar, implying that He is disarming Satan. Later, Jesus says that His death on the cross would render the final blow to Satan (John 12:31). Furthermore, in every instance where a person is mentioned as having an evil spirit, that spirit is cast out. So, in the ministry of Jesus, this is an enemy that is on a massive losing streak.

4. Our interaction with the enemy

(i) Authority
We have already seen in Chapter 22 that the Christian is to have authority over demons. From the start, Jesus delegates authority to the Twelve. We would necessarily exercise caution encouraging a new believer to do exactly what the disciples did, but essentially there is no reason why even a young Christian cannot both stand and take the offensive. Christ wants us to know that we, too, can have the same authority in His name (Luke 10:12,19).

(ii) Yes, but how?
I have no experience of dealing with people who exhibit signs of demon activity, but listening to those who do leads me to understand that the ministry of believers today is essentially the same as that practised by the disciples.

So imagine someone exhibits signs of a demon's activity, what would you do? You would check that appropriate measures have been taken to ensure that there is no medical condition that might account for the symptoms. You would then pray that God would be with you in what you are seeking to do, confessing anything that might hinder the filling of God's Spirit. Then expel the demon in the name of Jesus. There doesn't need to be any histrionics. The demon must leave at Christ's command. It is widely recognised as wise practice to work with other believers and it is of utmost importance that the person who has lost the demon seeks Christ's cleansing and filling with the Holy Spirit. Jesus tells us that expelled spirits may return with 'friends' and would make the person worse off (Luke 11:24–26).

(iii) Not cavalier

The victory of Christ over Satan and the demonic must not make the believer blasé however. Despite the authority of Christ over Satan, it is clear that the disciples were not immune to his advances. The apostle Peter goes from hero to zero in two verses. His declaration that Jesus was the Christ is seen as a 'revelation' (Matt. 16:16), but by verse 23, Jesus says 'Get behind me, Satan!' Furthermore, there were times when the disciples were not effective despite the authority they had been given (Matt. 17:16). Jesus tells them that they hadn't trusted in His ability to work and so had been left powerless.

Thus we have to always guard against two errors: the overestimation of Satan's power and the underestimation. The joke is told of a man who meets Satan standing outside a church. Satan looks upset. 'What's up?' asks the man. 'It's them in there,' says Satan, pointing to the church: 'They blame me for everything!'

(iv) No excuses

Having emphasised Satan's work, we note that there are many occasions when Christians have traditionally blamed Satan, even though God makes it clear that the source is elsewhere. The prime example is our personal sin. The devil is delighted whenever we behave outside of God's known will. In so doing we fail to enjoy the new kind of life, and settle for our way, setting a bad example for those looking on, and quenching God's work within us. But Jesus is clear that the remedy for sin is to do something about it, not shift the blame to Satan. Jesus tells us that the evil behaviour comes from evil hearts, which need renovation by His Spirit and our co-operation. For all the mention of the demonic in the Gospels, Jesus never claims that our sin can be excused as being down to Satan. Satan entering Judas is something Judas allows. The man who has a legion of demons is still able to fall at Jesus' feet. So if those oppressed by demons still have wills that are free to act, how much more we who are indwelt by the Spirit?

What Jesus didn't say

Some Christians have become obsessed with the demonic. Some talk and write about what they identify as 'territorial spirits' they believe can keep a whole nation in bondage. Others claim there are particular spirits that inflict people with particular sins (eg the spirit of jealousy). We are safer if we stick to Scripture. Yes demons are real and yes they have power, but at the name of Jesus they really do flee. Jesus didn't cast territorial demons out of say 'the Decapolis' or claim Mary Magdalene had a 'spirit of lust'. He just got on with the business of freeing people and positively proclaimed the kingdom of God. We should do the same. Remember, the devil is defeated.

Main points

- Jesus' mission is to confront and defeat Satan.
- Though 'defeated', he continues to be at work today.
- We can know victory over demons in Jesus' name as we operate with His power in His name.

Action

1. Read over the passages declaring Christ's victory over the enemy.
2. If necessary, spend time with a mature Christian and pray that any links in your past with demonic influences may be broken and Christ reign supreme.
3. Rejoice that your name is written in the Lamb's book of life.

Chapter 24

Persecution comes with the territory

When the first disciples signed up to be coached by Christ, He left them in no doubt that they were joining a battle. Jesus had faced the onslaught of the enemy at the beginning of His ministry, and conflict would punctuate the three years. So the disciples didn't have to read the small print to see what they were letting themselves in for, He told them straight: 'Blessed are you when people insult you, persecute you and falsely say all kinds of evil against you because of me' (Matt. 5:11). Later He said: 'If they persecuted me, they will persecute you also' (John 15:20). The word 'persecution' technically means 'any pressure that is brought to bear on individuals or a group because they are believers', but this explanation that persecution is all part of the package of being coached by Christ is surprising because of course Christ also says we are to enjoy a new kind of life. But in His mind there is no conflict. In answer to Peter's aggrieved statement in Mark 10:28, 'We have left everything to follow you!' Jesus says, '… no-one who has left home or brothers or sisters or mother or father or children or fields for me and the gospel will fail to receive a hundred times as much in this present age (homes, brothers, sisters, mothers, children and fields – and with them, persecutions) and in the age to come, eternal life.' Jesus is saying God will provide all you need, and when persecution comes, you needn't be surprised. Relax.

In some countries acknowledging that you are a Christian puts you on a hit list for ridicule, discrimination, beating, torture or death. Consider this:

- In North Korea tens of thousands of believers have been imprisoned for their faith and face torture, starvation and death.
- In parts of northern Nigeria, Christians' homes are torched, churches are razed to the ground.
- In Pakistan, Christians are denied jobs commensurate with their qualifications.
- There are at least 50 countries where overt persecution is taking place right now.
- There were more martyrs in the twentieth century than all other centuries combined. There is no sign that the twenty-first century is going to be any easier.
- *Foxe's Book of Martyrs* claims that as many as 250 million people are facing persecution of one sort or another, today. You won't read about it in your daily papers too often, but this is how many Christians live.

In the West we tend to be more tolerant, but even if the persecution is subtle, it is still there. All of which is news to some believers fed on a diet of 'everything will be fine now you are a Christian' material, which is a million miles away from Jesus' message. He never promised a rosy life, and those that do are misrepresenting the gospel.

So what does our Coach say to us about persecution?

1. Don't look for it

Some Christians behave in ways that provoke people to be angry. Jesus was not averse to saying things that were unpopular, but He didn't create unnecessary aggro. When He was asked whether it was right to pay taxes to Caesar, His clever answer, 'Give to Caesar what is Caesar's, and to God what is God's' (Matt. 22:21), demonstrated His acceptance of the ruling power, when a less clever answer could have created conflict. In the same way, the Church is wise to avoid areas of conflict with the State, while still being prepared to speak out when it needs to.

There are forms of evangelism that seem to ask for trouble. I was one of the workers in Victoria, London, who had to endure a man with a megaphone shouting at passers-by outside Victoria railway station most evenings for six months. Telling people they will 'die in their sins unless they trust in Christ', may have some orthodoxy about it, but it is hardly likely to create a true opportunity to explain what faith is about. Few listened, and maybe it was just as well. I admired his courage, but gave him low marks for communication. Our Coach has little sympathy for us when we are 'persecuted' because we are insensitive, lacking in good manners or make assumptions about our hearers. So if you receive persecution for being an idiot – best keep quiet about it, and learn for next time.

2. Be prepared to be shot at

The gospel is uncomfortable. It challenges people to reconsider the way they live. It calls people to repent. So it is no surprise that non-believers shoot the messenger. They will tell the messenger to be quiet, question the messenger's motives, argue that the messenger has no right to be delivering the message, suggest that the messenger has the wrong message, or that the message doesn't apply to them. Leith Samuel was a frequent missioner at university missions during his time with IVF (now UCCF). On one occasion he felt that things were not going well and so asked the students to pray for opposition. When they asked why he said, 'Because when there's opposition the truth becomes clearer!' So if you are being shot at, it can be good news – the message is getting through. In a country such as Britain, the bullets are subtle. It may be verbal: you are seen as arrogant, bigoted, old fashioned, stupid. It may mean that a work promotion is denied or that co-operation is not forthcoming. Christians that don't fit the sub-culture of smutty jokes, or financial malpractice are made to feel outsiders. But be wise – you may be 'persecuted' for the behaviour of other believers. When you admit to being a Christian, it is worth defining carefully what you mean, lest people label you as a type of Christian that is nothing like you. Being prepared to be shot at doesn't mean becoming game when the opposition is actually hunting something else. The gospel is an offence – we don't need to be.

3. Expect trouble at home

Persecution from friends and work colleagues is bad enough, but often the greatest pain is from those whom you would expect to be more understanding. Jesus said that His coming would divide some families.

> *'Do you think I came to bring peace on earth? No, I tell you, but division. From now on there will be five in one family divided against each other, three against two and two against three. They will be divided, father against son and son against father, mother against daughter and daughter against mother, mother-in-law against daughter-in-law and daughter-in-law against mother-in-law.'* (Luke 12:51–53)

This doesn't mean an intentional hostility; rather that following Jesus means He takes priority over the family units. In some Muslim and Hindu communities conversion to Christianity can lead to ostracism from the family and in some cases death. But it's also true in homes ostensibly Christian, especially if the parents feel their offspring's 'new faith' is suggesting that their 'faith' is invalid.

4. Rejoice if it comes

Jesus doesn't suggest that we should flee, or pray for persecution to stop, though both may be appropriate. He tells us to rejoice: 'Blessed are you when people insult you, persecute you and falsely say all kinds of evil against you because of me. Rejoice and be glad, because great is your reward in heaven, for in the same way they persecuted the prophets who were before you' (Matt. 5:11–12).

If we are persecuted, we stand in line with the prophets in the Old Testament who declared the Word of God but suffered for it. We rejoice because of the privilege of being numbered with them and because God notices and will reward us, both in giving us a sense of His presence in this life, but also in the next when all wrongs are righted and God rewards those who are faithful to Him. It is worth stating that God gives us special grace at such times. You may not be able to imagine such behaviour and certainly it will test your growth, but God draws near to those who face the tough trials. In Acts, this very thing happened. After being beaten, we read, the apostles rejoiced that 'they had been counted worthy of suffering disgrace for the Name' (Acts 5:41). The reasons to rejoice may sound odd, and we might struggle to imagine ourselves rejoicing in this way. But they reflect the new kind of life that Jesus promises. Persecution reminds us of the distinction between this world and the next and elicits a response, which we can't generate ourselves, but reflects the life of God within us.

When the writer of Hebrews writes of Jesus anticipating the cross, he says, '… who for the joy set before him endured the cross, scorning its shame …' (Heb. 12:2). There is a special joy that comes when we anticipate the glory we will enjoy even when we suffer in the present. The rejoicing of the persecuted is a powerful witness. Many have found Christ because of what they saw in the lives of the people they were torturing. It is here that the new kind of life is seen so clearly, as believers follow their Master in praying for their captors as Christ prayed, 'Father, forgive them, for they do not know what they are doing.' They know that their own suffering is temporary, but the captors' suffering will be eternal if they don't receive forgiveness from God.

5. Don't be fearful

Along with joy, the disciples were not to be fearful of persecution. We see in the Gospels there was pressure on Jesus and the disciples at various times. In Nazareth, Jesus was threatened by a mob (Luke 4:28–30) and at times provoked angry reactions. But in the main, the common people heard Him gladly, and it is not until His final week that the pressure builds. But although they faced pressure, I don't imagine the Twelve nervously watching their backs in case they were attacked. The spirit among the Twelve was not morbid, if anything they were more upbeat than they should have been, struggling to grasp that their Master would soon die. James and John's request for preferment (Mark 10:35) comes after Jesus has explained that He must go to the cross

This command not to fear is expanded in Luke 12:4–12. When Jesus predicts a time when the disciples would face courts, He tells them not to worry what they will say, for the Holy Spirit will give them words. In some places persecution is experienced at a level Christians in the West can barely imagine. Nevertheless, whether the persecution is obvious on a daily basis, or irregular and subtler, Jesus intends that His kingdom will advance. Christians in persecuted countries are concerned that Christians in parts of the 'West' face so little persecution that they have become half-hearted as a result. Odd though it may seem, they pray for the West.

What Jesus didn't say

Ever heard a Christian say that things are going so badly that he or she 'must be doing something right'? It may be a reasonable conclusion, when unexpected things befall people which prevent the communication of Christian truth, but often it's nothing more than poor planning, overwork or foolish decisions that have caused the problem. On the other hand, some believers seem to quake at the first sign of trouble. They seem to expect that God is not in it if it doesn't go smoothly. The search for spiritual meaning behind events is an awkward business. All we can be sure of is that spiritual progress is often made in the face of opposition. The apostle Paul told the Ephesian believers that our fight is not against flesh and blood. So when you do face any opposition, remember who is really opposing you, and that he is defeated.

Main points

- Persecution will come to you at some point.
- Don't invite it unnecessarily, and don't be fearful.
- Rejoice that God is allowing you to suffer.

Action

1. Think of times when you have felt pressure or persecution. How did you react? Can you imagine yourself rejoicing? (If you

haven't sensed persecution yet, determine now that you will lean on God and allow Him to teach you through it and love those who have it in for you.)

2. Find out more about persecuted believers and determine to pray for them.

Chapter 25

Tough times are inevitable

'No pain, no gain' is a mantra that is heard on the lips of many sports coaches. It is literally true. When you use muscles you have not used for a while or try a new exercise or training technique, it is normal to feel a dull ache of soreness in the muscles that were trained. This pain is caused by microscopic tears in the fibres of the connective tissues in your body – the ligaments that connect bones to other bones, and the tendons that connect muscles to bones. This may sound harmful but is in fact the natural response of your muscles when they experience work. Coaches say this is why it is so important that you get enough rest between specific muscle workouts. Each time you work out with weights, or push your body in exercise, you cause this 'damage' – these tiny tears in your muscles; they need ample resting time to rebuild and become even stronger, bigger and firmer.

The mantra is true also as the sportspeople push themselves mentally to accomplish greater feats. Golfers overcome nerves to play well in spite of knowing that every shot counts. Tennis players learn to not 'choke' when facing a key point. Middle distance double Olympic gold winner, Sebastian Coe, was once asked to comment on the potential of a young runner and said: 'He hasn't learned how to hurt himself.'

Some Christians act as if the mantra can be directly applied to spiritual growth. If life is unpleasant then God must be teaching you something. If things are going smooth, don't worry, disaster awaits around the corner! It is true that Jesus taught that suffering was a necessary part of the Christian life; however, He studiously avoided the unhealthy stereotypes we can be tempted to adopt.

From His coaching a number of things are clear:

1. Jesus suffered that one day we might be free from suffering

Jesus tells the Twelve, 'For even the Son of Man did not come to be served, but to serve, and to give his life as a ransom for many' (Mark 10:45). We have noted already that the central message of Jesus was His announcement of the kingdom of God, that God's reign had entered our world in His life and ministry overlapping and contrasting with the world, what we have called the 'new kind of life'. The Jews awaited the end of the world for the alleviation of suffering, but Jesus was telling them that they could know God's reign now. In Luke 4 we receive a summary of why Jesus came: 'good news to the poor, release to the captives, sight to the blind.' So throughout Jesus' ministry we see His compassion towards those who were hurting and a willingness to bring relief.

Hence it is a surprise to many followers of Jesus today that suffering is part of their lives at all. They assume that God blots out pain before it affects them and forget that Jesus Himself tells the story of the way in which many receive His Word gladly, but the cares of this life choke the Word and it doesn't take root. People fail to realise the way the kingdom works. Yes, God intervenes, but the ministry of Jesus gives glimpses of the day when evil will be finally ended, it did not mean that life for Him or His followers was pain-free. His task was not to glide through life in a hermetically-sealed bubble, but to enter our world as a genuine person, identifying with us in our pain. We read that He was tired and thirsty and hungry and of course He faced the most vicious and savage beating at the hands of the Roman guards before the agony of crucifixion itself. It was at the cross that He put a potential end to suffering for all who would put their confidence in Him. The greatest suffering was spiritual as

He suffered the wrath of God against our sin that we would not need to. He suffered so that one day we would be free of all suffering.

So our Coach knows the pain we face. He calls us to live close to God, despite the distractions and disappointments of life, because He has done it Himself.

2. Suffering goes with the territory

Jesus told the Twelve that there were tough times ahead: they were hounded out of synagogues and some were put to death (John 16:1–4). Historical records suggest that John is the only apostle to die of old age. Jesus knew that His own life would end with an extraordinary period of pain, both physical and spiritual, and that those following would have to accept this would be possible. Chapter 24 focused upon the persecution believers will face. A suffering-free Christianity is not true Christianity.

3. Some suffering is self-inflicted

We have already seen that self-denial is part of the new life in Christ. This self-denial, though apparently painful, leads us to joy as we learn how the new kind of life is so much better than the old one. The parable of the pearl merchant in Matthew 13:45–46 reminds us that it is no hardship to give up a life heading for ruin to enjoy the wonders of the kingdom. Yes, it may have hurt a little to 'sell all he had', but this was because he appreciated the worth of the pearl. But pain is self-inflicted when we fail to realise the glorious opportunity of fellowship with Christ by His Spirit. I inflict pain on myself when I want my own way, for I fail to enjoy the purposes of God in my life. When we violate the laws of life that God has laid down we cause ourselves pain, just as surely as dropping a hammer on our toe.

When Jesus anticipated Peter's denial He told him He would pray for him, that his faith would not fail. Interestingly, He doesn't give him a pep talk, or 'five ways to avoid denying Me', but allows Him to live His life and face the consequences, painful though they were. In due course He would re-instate Peter and assure him of his key role in the life of the fledgling Church.

4. Some suffering is part of our growth

When cyclist, Lance Armstrong, spoke at a conference in Portland, Oregon, after he won the 1999 Tour de France bike race, he said to the audience: 'If I had to choose between getting testicular cancer and winning the Tour de France, I would choose testicular cancer.'

He went on to explain how he had changed for the better after battling an advanced form of testicular cancer, which kept him out of cycling for nearly two years. He described the cancer as 'a special wake-up call' and has set up a Foundation to help people survive the disease.

Our instinctive reaction to suffering is to want to get as far away from it as possible. We find it hard to imagine ourselves welcoming it, or arranging for it. But that's exactly what Jesus advocates when He calls us to learn to be like Him. We have noted earlier that fasting was a part of the life of Jesus and should be 'enjoyable' as we grow to sense closeness to God during it. But it may not be so the first time we do it. I recall a real reluctance when my boss urged the church to fast when I was part of the staff team and I wonder whether I would have done so if I didn't feel obliged to set an example! Fasting is not the only discipline that may seem tough at first. Any practice within the new life has an element of 'suffering'; activities such as praying out loud for the first time, sharing our faith with someone who is apathetic, reading the Bible at the end of a busy day, inviting a newcomer to lunch, may all have an element of difficulty and unpleasantness. Yet we know they are the right thing to do and ask God that we might do them out of hearts that are truly willing.

When it feels tough we can recall the words of the Twelve when many disciples left Jesus because His teaching had become too hard. Jesus asked the Twelve whether they intended to stay. They replied, 'To whom shall we go? You have the words of eternal life' (John 6:68). Sure it was tough to go on, but it was tougher to bail out. The well-known cliché, 'don't become bitter, but become better' is literally true. Our tough circumstances are prime opportunities for us to grow.

5. Suffering points us to a better future

Jesus does not give a reasoned explanation for suffering in His teaching. But He gives an important insight into the way we should understand it in Luke 13:1–5. Here He replies to questioning about some deaths in Jerusalem that had become front-page news. Jesus explains that we should not try and assess whether the people deserved to die. They were not 'worse sinners' than those that lived. But 'unless you repent, you too will all perish'. Their death was a reminder that life is short and fragile and so we need to be prepared to meet God when He calls us. Physical suffering and death are a reminder of the suffering we will face in the next world if we do not repent. As C.S. Lewis put it, 'Pain insists upon being attended to, God whispers to us in our pleasures, speaks in our conscience, but shouts in our pains. It is his megaphone to rouse a deaf world.'[1]

The better future we are promised is not just after death. Jesus promises that no one who has left his or her family will fail to receive more in this life and along with this, eternal life (Mark 10:29–31). God has His way of providing people within the Christian community who perform the filial roles that we may have surrendered when we came to faith.

5. Suffering does not equal virtue

As we noted in the introduction to this chapter, some Christians seem to assume that suffering must come. For them, times of blessing and pleasantness are only partially enjoyed because of the fear that suffering must be around the corner. We can acknowledge that we will suffer because we are fallen people in a fallen world and that God can use it to His glory, but that doesn't mean that suffering is a virtue. A Christianity that assumes disaster must be around the corner has misread God and His purposes of love and joy for His people. There will be times when we may have to accept the pain and rejoice in the Lord, but that doesn't mean we can't do all that's sensible to alleviate the pain in us and others. We can 'gain' without pain too.

WHAT JESUS DIDN'T SAY

For the Christian who believes God to be all-powerful, suffering can represent big problems. Why doesn't He intervene in my life? we ask. Why does He allow a young bride to be killed in an accident? Why does an evangelist get ill with cancer? Ultimately there are no answers. We would like life to be smooth and fair and it's not. But just because it is not going well, it doesn't mean God has forgotten us, or diminished His love for us. Our faith is being stretched and that's no bad thing.

MAIN POINTS

- Suffering will be part of your Christian life.
- God will work in your suffering to draw you closer to Him and confirm your faith to you.
- Don't assume the worst must happen.

ACTION

1. List the suffering in your life. What could you do to alleviate it? What do you need to ask God to do?
2. List the good things about the suffering. Tell God how you feel about it.
3. Thank Jesus that He understands what suffering is and can help us with any trial we face.

Note

1. C.S. Lewis, *The Problem of Pain* (HarperCollins, 2002).

Chapter 26

If you want your wealth that much, then keep it!

Ask most Christians, what was Jesus' view of wealth and you would get the same answer: 'He wasn't impressed with it.' Jesus was from a humble and poor background, brought up to work as a carpenter, in a family who could only afford the poorest offering when attending the Temple. He left His employment to begin His ministry and told His disciples to leave theirs; we know of four fishermen and a tax collector who left regular income to join up. He was angry at the moneychangers at the Temple and seemed to be on the side of the poor with His words: 'Blessed are the poor.' The whole tenor of His teaching is that we should pass by the wealth of this world, knowing that treasures are laid up for us in the world to come.

Many argue that this is so clear as to be unarguable. But there are churches throughout the world and even in the Third World who preach a very different message, claiming that Jesus taught that Christians should look to God for riches, His intention being that some of the wealth in the world to come be enjoyed now as a testimony to God's faithfulness. They rail against what they see as a poverty mentality arguing that if we only had greater faith we would see more material blessing.

So which is correct? Do both sides have a point? Are both wrong? What does our Coach tell us about wealth?

From Jesus' coaching we find the following:

1. Riches can keep you from the kingdom

On one occasion a rich ruler asks Jesus what he needs to do to follow Him (Mark 10:17). Jesus tells him to sell all he has, give to the poor and follow Him. Although a law keeper (so he thought), he was unable to detach himself from the riches that in his case were the barrier to him following Jesus. Jesus was always clear that we forsake all to follow Him. His words to the rich man were a surprise to His disciples who assumed, with the rest of Israel, that the rich were rich because of God's blessing and were thus prime candidates for the kingdom of God. Hence their response 'Who then can be saved?'

The understanding that riches can be a barrier to entering the kingdom is further explored in the parable of the rich fool. The farmer builds bigger barns because of his success, only to discover that it's the last day of his life and he has not made provision for the world to come (Luke 12:15–21).

Jesus is critical of the religious leaders of the day who were crazy about money (Luke 16:15). Riches are deceptive, because the ease and comfort they bring can delude us into overlooking the precariousness of life. No investment portfolio can shield us from death. Following His criticism of the Pharisees, Jesus gives a graphic picture of the after life, in Luke 16:19–31, contrasting Lazarus, who goes to 'Abraham's side', with a rich man in torment in hell – a frightening picture of the uselessness of this world's material benefits in the light of the world to come. When Jesus speaks of the sort of faith that possesses the kingdom He uses the metaphor of the man who finds great treasure and the man who finds a pearl. In both cases the man in question sold all he had that he might possess what he wanted.

So our Coach asks us whether we love our wealth more than we love Him. Wealth is one of the things that we cannot cling onto if we are taking up our cross and following Him.

2. Put serving Christ above riches

But having come to faith, we still need to beware of the dangers of wealth. Jesus tells the Twelve that what you see is not what you get, when it comes to wealth: 'Do not store up for yourselves treasures on earth ... But store up for yourselves treasures in heaven ...' (Matt. 6:19).

Treasures on earth have the pretence of durability, backed by marketing campaigns, but fade away with the next model – followers of Jesus build up a heavenly investment that will not pass away.

Directly after encouraging the disciples not to worry about food and clothing, Jesus says: 'Do not be afraid, little flock, for your Father has been pleased to give you the kingdom. Sell your possessions and give to the poor. Provide purses for yourselves that will not wear out, a treasure in heaven that will not be exhausted, where no thief comes near and no moth destroys. For where your treasure is, there your heart will be also' (Luke 12:32–34). When Jesus sent His disciples out to announce the kingdom of God, He explicitly tells them not to take money with them. They were to depend upon the generosity of the people they went to.

The Twelve could know an assurance that all would be well in this life. Their provision was met by their heavenly Father. He provides for our needs and often for our wants too. When I was based in a church in Bournemouth, I visited a missionary based at Wycliffe Bible Translators, Germany. She showed us a paper outlining the Mission's stance towards money. It urges its staff never to say, 'We can't afford it', but rather, 'Let's see if God intends us to have it'. For a while I had no regular salary. It was no hardship to depend on my wife's teaching salary but it was amazing to see how God provided during, and sometimes before, a financial crisis.

This is not suggesting that if you give up your job, God will provide; earning a salary is God's means of provision for most people. Our Coach is saying that we shouldn't put the need for finances above serving Him. This trust in God rather than wealth has led to believers making career choices based on service and not salary. Would-be ministers and missionaries have left high paid jobs and attractive benefits to serve the kingdom. People have opted not to take a promotion because it would take time from their ministry outside the workplace, or mean uprooting from a church where they serve. Some have literally lived by faith, depending on God to provide their needs.

3. Judge yourself by God's standards and not the culture

Jesus says, 'Watch out! Be on your guard against all kinds of greed; a man's life does not consist in the abundance of his possessions' (Luke 12:15).

In Jesus' day the rich were seen as the beneficiaries of the blessing of God; the size of house you owned and the clothes you wore gave a standing in society. The Gospels teach a countercultural attitude to wealth. Christians don't see their status in terms of the size of their salary, their purchasing power or net worth. Their understanding that 'a man's life does not consist in the abundance of his possessions', stops them making judgments about people on the basis of apparent income. They are also more keenly aware of the folly of advertising campaigns that do not focus on the qualities and usefulness of the product but the perceived lifestyle benefits it brings or the feelings of 'status' or high self-image they purport to engender. Modern advertising campaigns presume that we will break the commandment, 'Do not covet'. It is a short journey from watching a TV advert to coveting what your neighbour has. But coveting ruins relationships. I am made to feel inferior because of what I don't own and become jealous of the person who does have it. All of which is crazy, because in God's kingdom God is looking after me. I trust Him, why would I want what someone else has? I can be pleased for them and, if really necessary, pray about whether I should have it too; but why covet?

4. Be careful how wealth is accumulated

So what does Jesus say to us in a modern market economy?

Wealth is not evil. Christian businesspeople make sure they follow the new kind of life as they operate in the workplace. Principles of fairness, honesty, providing value for money should characterise a Christian business. In one business run by a Christian, the owner has insisted that the employees have a share in the business. Which wouldn't sound so unusual if the business weren't in Malaysia, where employees have never owned shares before!

Christians with a rare skill or talent find employers beat a path to their door offering good salaries and bonus schemes. Honest endeavour, a love of fellow colleagues, a willingness to speak the truth, forgiveness when wronged will generally hold a person in good stead. Christian wealth is not a sin.

Some acquire wealth by saving and investing wisely. Providing for one's dependants in old age is prudent and appropriate, especially in an age of credit cards where the temptation is to buy and live for the moment rather than save for a rainy day. Jesus does not condemn rich Christians, He just wants them to be wise in their stewardship and not fail to value Him more than their wealth – that would be financial disaster.

5. Don't presume on God, but don't ignore Him either

So what of those churches who believe that wealth is God's purpose for His people? What can we say?

(a) Many believers will be wealthy and successful by virtue of being Christians. Sociologists have identified what is known as redemptive lift. A person becomes a Christian, so they give up spending money on cigarettes, alcohol and gambling. They find that their work life is affected, since they serve the Lord and not men. The developing character qualities mean they follow through on promises, don't waste company time and money. The employer notices their better output and attitude and so gives them a raise, or a promotion. The money saved, plus the raise increases their disposable income, and that income is spent more wisely. Greater wealth and prosperity will come as a result of becoming a Christian in some cases.

(b) The argument that God wants us all to be wealthy is dangerous nonsense. Having said that God may bless us with wealth because of character change, and in order to further His purposes, it is palpable nonsense to suggest that wealth is God's intention for every believer, or that poverty is connected to a lack of faith. Churches typically preach this message because they believe God's material blessing of Israel applies to the Church today, forgetting that the New Testament covenant has rendered certain patterns of activity obsolete now that Christ has come. Some within the churches are blessed materially for the reasons already given, but to promise riches and any other physical benefit is to write a cheque that God is not prepared to honour, and is an insult to believers worldwide who have been faithful with little. Jesus made it clear that the poor were welcome into the kingdom, and, for all the possibilities of material advancement, never promises that they will be wealthy.

What Jesus doesn't say

No one can claim that Jesus favours a particular economic system, though some have tried. Jesus is concerned primarily with calling us to a new life in His kingdom, not with producing a list of laws that we must apply in any and every situation. We are learning from Jesus how He would live if He were us. So He trusts that as we develop His character, we will apply this to our working life and use of money. If we run a business it will be as a Christian. If we handle money it will be as a Christian. So we will have a countercultural view of wealth, which will challenge every economy, business owner and employee. Jesus doesn't specifically tackle master–slave relationships, for example, but the epistles do, arguing for the two parties to behave with each other as Christians – masters with fairness, slaves with endeavour. The teaching of Jesus undermines the very notion of one person owning another. Whatever the economic climate we find ourselves in, and however real or perceived the injustices are, we are to live as children of the King; using wealth wisely, honouring God above all and rejoicing to see the way in which He multiplies our efforts and gifts.

Main points

- Riches can keep you from the kingdom and hinder your growth when in it.
- You should have a different attitude to riches. You can afford to be generous.
- Wealth is not evil, though take care how it is accumulated.
- Wealth is not promised to the believer.

Action

1. Think of the people you imagine are the richest and poorest

you know. Now imagine that their wealth was reversed. Do you think of them any differently?

2. Consider how many decisions you agonise over because of money? Does this make money more important than it should be, or is this just being wise?

Chapter 27

Money is the root of all kinds of good

When talking to church leaders about the financial life of a church, Bill Hybels, senior pastor of Willow Creek Community Church, Chicago, asks the question, 'How much ministry can you do for $100?' He answers the question himself: 'About $100 worth.'

Church buildings, staff salaries/stipends, all require money from somewhere. If the giving of your local church stopped overnight, the place would probably have to see some changes by next month and major changes by next year, if not sooner. Furthermore, the ability of a church to meet the needs outside the church also requires funds, by and large.

God's kingdom is not measured by the dollars or pounds spent. His Spirit does not wait for fund-raising committees to meet their targets. Worldwide the Church that is poorest is seeing the greatest growth. Nevertheless, the reality is that many churches and Christian organisations would tell you that they could do a lot more for the kingdom if they had more money.

Of Jesus' 38 parables 16 focus on how to handle money and possessions, and it has been calculated that 15 per cent of Jesus' recorded words are on the subject of money, so what does our Coach tell us about our giving?

1. Develop a giving mentality

The new kind of life revolution is especially demonstrated when it comes to giving of money to serve the Church and those in need. As a child of the kingdom you are loved by God who is committed to provide for your needs. Excited by His resources and enjoying His bounty, you can have a new attitude to wealth, as we saw in the last chapter. Love compels you to provide for others; you give money, or loan property with joyful abandon, conscious that you can do so much good for the Church and those wider afield. You do not so identify yourself with your goods that you possess them in a way that excludes their use by other people. This may not sound like you, but the very first lesson from our Coach concerns developing a giving mentality; it's the mentality that caused the early disciples to sell all they had when a local problem in Jerusalem demanded it.

2. Have some to give away

The whole subject of giving assumes the basic point that we have sufficient wealth to meet our needs in order to have a surplus. So in Luke we read that women supported Jesus out of their own wealth, including Joanna, the wife of Chuza, the manager of Herod's household, which raises the intriguing possibility that Herod's wages may have partly financed Jesus' work! With 13 to feed daily, that represented a considerable financial commitment.

When Jesus' body was removed from the cross it was placed in a tomb owned by Joseph of Arimathea. If Joseph hadn't owned a tomb the body of Jesus would have been thrown on a rubbish tip with the others and so there would have been no empty tomb indicating Christ's resurrection.

In the Early Church we have the example of Barnabas who sold a field to provide money for the believers.

I am very happy that there are those who make a living from the gospel, as long as we remember that there need to be those who are making 'more than a living' to support this work. It is a little rich (pun intended) when those that depend on the giving of their supporters and church members then rail against those same people for making too much money!

To have some to give away may represent a considerable step for some. Credit Action calculate that 40 per cent of people in the UK have debts (in addition to mortgage debt), of £3,000, and the figure is not much different between Christians and those who aren't! (March 2004 figures). One large church calculates that it takes the average new believer three years from conversion to the point where they are ready to give regularly to the church.

Jesus never made judgments about people who had wealth. Wealth in and of itself is not a sin. The truth is there is no virtue in poverty per se. A poor person can be just as obsessed with wealth as a rich person. In their case, the desire to be wealthy blinds them to the kingdom.

Ironically, it is sometimes the wealthy who are more open to the good news of the kingdom because having got to the top of the tree, or been born into wealth, they know money can't buy happiness! Whether a person is rich or poor materially makes little difference to their standing before God. Both the rich and the poor need to put their trust exclusively in Christ. So when Jesus says, 'Blessed are the poor', He is not saying become poor 'in order' to get in the kingdom, but rather that when it comes to the kingdom, the poor whom the world typically despises, can be blessed. Similarly, the rich are not cursed, but are advised not to reckon on their riches meaning they will be OK in the life to come.

3. Be generous

The Old Testament principle of tithing is not something Jesus spoke much about. He mentions the way the Pharisees were fastidious about tithing every little thing they owned, and by implication encouraged it (Matt. 23:23) but He nowhere insists every disciple must tithe. The rest of the New Testament encourages cheerful giving but not tithing as such. Having said that, it is a useful principle. If we gave 10 per cent under the old covenant, should we give less under the new?

Those who are wealthy are encouraged to be generous. And in God's eyes, the small gift from the widow (Luke 21:1–4) is just as valued as the larger gift from the millionaire. It is clear that we give to God. It is an act of trust that should we need what we have given, He will provide. Anyone who takes the feeding of the 5,000 seriously will recognise that God has no problem providing abundantly, and if the major focus of that miracle is upon the spiritual lesson that Jesus later draws, that doesn't mean there isn't also a material lesson regarding God's practical provision.

Sadly, churches in Britain have become afraid to talk about money. When they do it is along the lines of 'We are looking to the Lord to provide.' This is all very well, but of course God uses people. To my knowledge He has never performed a miracle of multiplying cash. I'm not sure that Jesus telling Peter where he would find their tax payment in a fish quite counts, remarkable though it was.

So to set aside workers for service at home and abroad, maintain church buildings, provide evangelistic literature, means someone parting with a proportion of their wealth to free it up for kingdom use. Jesus encourages an attitude towards life and the kingdom that makes the financial support of kingdom life thoroughly normal.

4. Give in secret

The giving of money and possessions has become popular in some circles. As well as benefiting your charity, you have the added kudos of being seen to be generous. Jesus is clear that God is not impressed. 'You have received your reward in full' (Matt. 6:2). You did it to gain applause and that's exactly what you got. But don't expect God to join in. There's a world of difference between signalling your gift with a fanfare and the appropriate and sensible declaration of a gift for purposes, so that the recipient can benefit from Gift Aid (in the UK). Some Christian organisations tailor their fundraising strategy to target certain givers of course! The point is this – only you and the treasurer generally need to know what is given.

5. Be shrewd

One passage of Jesus' teaching that has been misunderstood is His parable of the shrewd manager (Luke 16:1–9). This shrewd manager (employee) was sacked for incompetence and so promptly reduced the debts of the business owner's creditors to ingratiate himself with them.

Jesus says, 'I tell you, use worldly wealth to gain friends for yourselves, so that when it is gone, you will be welcomed into eternal dwellings ... So if you have not been trustworthy in handling worldly wealth, who will trust you with true riches?' (Luke 16:9, 11).

It is a difficult passage and so I am cautious in my interpretation. It is hard to fathom why Jesus seems to commend a man who doesn't treat his own boss well, having deserved the sack! Insight may be found when we realise that the debts he reduced may have been the interest payments charged, payments that were unnecessarily high. Hence the steward is potentially helping his own Master's relationship with his creditors, as well as his own future employment prospects. What is clear is that Jesus is commending the use of wealth to benefit people. He is also reminding us that there is some link between how we use wealth in this world and our responsibilities in the new heavens and earth, where we will still be active, albeit as sinless people in an environment free from sin.

The shrewd approach is important. To illustrate this I want to consider the question, if you have £10,000 is it better to give it all away, or manage it for the benefit of others? The first takes a few seconds, the latter is an ongoing responsible activity which might last years. There will be times when both activities might be appropriate, but we shouldn't assume that the giving away option is necessarily the most godly, for there will be times when keeping and managing the wealth for others will be the more spiritually costly option.

6. Prepare for eternity

The British prime minister in the 1980s, Margaret Thatcher, once used the parable of the talents (Matt. 25:14ff.) to justify a free market approach to the economy. This is certainly a misuse of the passage, which is primarily concerned, with our use of spiritual gifts prior to the Master's return. Nevertheless, there is a parallel for the Christian, and clear indications that our faithfulness in this world will have a bearing on our work in the next. In the parable of the minas (Luke 19:11–27), faithfulness in handling wealth is rewarded with management of heavenly resources (cities) in the new heavens and new earth. It is as if Jesus says, 'You have done well, take Paris,

Moscow, LA, Cape Town and Shanghai.' We give because God has given to us, but we also give because of our faith in God to provide. If Jesus is happy that this be seen as an incentive, then who am I to argue?

What Jesus didn't say

Jesus never minded talking about money so it shouldn't be a big problem in the Church. Yes, it can be a snare. We can worship it rather than God and we can give the impression that we are after visitors' money when they come to church. But it also a blessing, it enables us to do things. Earning it and using it is a great blessing. Often the poorest churches financially are the most generous givers. God doesn't want His work hamstrung by low funds and poor equipment, and His servants scrambling around trying to make ends meet.

Main points

- You should develop a generous spirit.
- Use what you have wisely so that the kingdom benefits.
- Remember that heavenly treasure lasts.

Action

1. Give what you can when you can. Pray as you do so. Don't worry if you start small. If you can't manage 10 per cent aim for a figure you can manage, and do it cheerfully.
2. Ask God to increase your generosity.
3. Use the influence you have to help take things to a new level, in your church and any Christian organisations you are part of.

PART SIX

Enjoy your future with Him

Our belief that the new kind of life is to be lived now does not hide the fact that the best is yet to be. We would be very miserable if this were all there were, exciting though it is to be part of Christ's adventure.

Christ reminds us that there is a judgment to be aware of. He spends a long time on it and we need to be clear what to expect. He also excites us about His return and the glorious kingdom as the new heavens and the new earth are unveiled in all their glory.

The new kind of life anticipates this glory, but you also have to live tomorrow. It's great to know that you have a highly competent guide who can navigate the journey with you.

Chapter 28

Heaven would be hell for those who don't know God

Ian Thorpe was regarded as a near certainty for Olympic Gold in his best event, the 400-metre freestyle swimming. However, to be selected for the Olympic team to go to Athens in 2004, he needed to win at his country's trials. He's the fastest in the world so it was thought that nothing could stop him – except himself that is. At the start of the qualifying heat Thorpe toppled off his starting blocks into the pool and, under the strict regulations governing the event, was disqualified.

Rules are rules, and however bizarre they may seem, the Australian Olympic committee had to disqualify Thorpe, despite the fact that they knew he was not seeking to gain an advantage. This caused a great furore which eventually led to pressure being put on the swimmer who qualified, but had little chance of a medal, to give up his place so that Thorpe could represent Australia in this event, as well as others he'd qualified for.

A look at the judgment of God is a necessary part of our coaching. We need to be clear about God's judgment of our friends and family, and what if anything awaits us. Understanding the rules, and the penalty for infraction is a necessary part of the process. And this time the rules are fair and just.

So what does our Coach say about judgment?

The theme of God's judgment is peppered throughout the Bible. In judgment, God calls people to account for their behaviour and decides on the appropriate outcomes. God punishes Adam and Eve and all their descendants with spiritual and then physical death when they rebel in the Garden of Eden. God intervenes at various points in the Old Testament narrative; the destruction of the wicked through the Flood; the destruction of the inhabitants of Sodom and Gomorrah; Israel's punishment of nations, notably the Canaanites by Joshua; the punishment of Israel at various times as their enemies overrun them; the defeat and capture of Israel and Judah by Assyria and Babylon respectively.

Judgment is also a theme of the teaching of Jesus. He speaks of God's judgment on Israel (Matt. 11:20–24; Mark 12:1–12; Luke 11:47–51), where time to change was limited (Luke 13:6–9). The Jewish leaders received particular rebuke (Matt. 23:29–36). He speaks of the major judgment when God will intervene in human history and execute final judgment when He establishes His kingdom in its fullness (Matt. 25:31–32).

We are told that all of our lives will come under scrutiny. 'There is nothing concealed that will not be disclosed, or hidden that will not be made known. What you have said in the dark will be heard in the daylight, and what you have whispered in the ear in the inner rooms will be proclaimed from the roofs' (Luke 12:2–3).

We need to be clear first of all that the Christian's condemnation has been taken by Jesus. Although we deserve God's wrath for our sin, He bore God's wrath when He died so that those who have faith in Him will not perish/come under condemnation. The judgment has two ultimate outcomes: Those who reject Christ face God's wrath, those who trust Him are welcomed to the new kind of life in this world and the presence of God in the next.

Many believers are concerned to know what will happen to the vast numbers who have never heard the gospel. There are no categoric statements by Jesus on what will happen to those who have never heard about His life and death. Some believe that a hint is given when He speaks of degrees of punishment. When He speaks about the cities who refused to repent at His teaching, He contrasts their 'culpability' with those who had not had the advantage of hearing the gospel. Jesus says: '… it will be more bearable for Tyre and Sidon on the day of judgment than for you' (Matt 11:22). Jesus also says, 'From everyone who has been given much, much will be demanded' (Luke 12:48). So it is suggested that people will be judged according to the light they had and what they did with the light they had.

John Stott, author and former rector of All Souls, Langham Place, said:

> I believe the most Christian stance is to remain agnostic on this question … The fact is that God, alongside the most solemn warnings about our responsibility to respond to the gospel, has not revealed how he will deal with those who have never heard it. We have to leave them in the hands of the God of infinite mercy and justice, who manifested these qualities most fully in the cross. Abraham's question, 'will not the Judge of all the earth do right?' (Genesis 18:25) is our confidence too.[1]

Judgment has a glorious outcome for Christians who have served faithfully.

When speaking of the faithful servants who used their talents, Jesus says: 'You shall have authority over ten cities' (Luke 19:17,19; Matt. 25:31–46). It can be dangerous to draw too much from a parable, but this indicates some degrees of reward in the after life, though it's worth remembering that there will be no jealousy or regret. We won't spend eternity wishing things had been different or resenting our place. We will be delighted to be there and delighted with the rewards everyone receives.

Hell

Jesus' teaching on hell is regarded by some as a contentious subject. Hell is specifically promised for those who: reject Jesus (Matt. 11:20–24; Luke 10:12–15; 12:8–9); reject the prophets (Matt. 23:31–33); are hypocrites (Matt. 23:15,33); use hateful language and intent (Matt. 5:22); are unfaithful (Matt. 24:45–51); unrepentant (Matt. 5:29–30; 18:8–9); disobedient (Matt. 5:22; 7:19; 13:40,42,50; John 15:6). In short, all who deliberately reject the way of Christ.

So what should we understand about hell?

Some theologians suggest that hell is a place where people will be punished for a limited time, according to the degree of their wickedness. They argue that the language used to describe hell fits this understanding. They say the image of a fire that burns up, suggests that after the person is burned they are no more. For example: 'Into the eternal fire prepared for the devil and his angels' (Matt. 25:41). There is also destruction (Matt. 7:19; 13:40, 42, 50; John 15:6).

According to this view, our immortality is dependent upon our taking the life Jesus offers. Those who resist will face death and be effectively snuffed out. Punishment is real and unpleasant, but limited. This understanding sounds more palatable than the traditional view that hell is eternal conscious punishment for the wicked, but it doesn't square with the balance of Scripture. Consider these descriptions:

Jesus says: 'And cast the worthless servant into the outer darkness; there men will weep and gnash their teeth' (Matt. 25:30, RSV). He speaks of 'unquenchable fire' (Mark 9:43, RSV), 'where their worm does not die, and the fire is not quenched' (Mark 9:48, RSV). He calls hell: 'this place of torment' (Luke 16:28). 'Depart from me, you who are cursed, into the eternal fire prepared for the devil and his angels' (Matt. 25:41). The parable of the rich man and Lazarus depicts the man in torment concerned to warn his family not to come. He also says: 'Then they will go away to eternal punishment, but the righteous to eternal life' (Matt. 25:46).

These passages suggest punishment without end. In Matthew 25:46 the words about eternal life are set directly against eternal punishment, implying that if one is eternal, so is the other.

I can't deny that there are no philosophical difficulties with this teaching. To us, the punishment probably seems excessive and we struggle to understand a punishment that goes on endlessly. But the truth is that we have a very poor grasp of who deserves what. We are sentimental and fail to see evil as it is. The spurning of the love of God seems a little thing to us. We know that God is loving and merciful and righteous and will do whatever brings Him glory within His world, and so in these matters we trust Him, making sure that we do all we can to keep people from facing such a dreadful future. Furthermore, no one will be in hell who hasn't chosen a course distant from God. Indeed for them, heaven might be like 'hell'. If they were to come to 'the banquet' unprepared they would feel completely out of place and not be able to stand the glory of God that burns against sin (Matt. 22:12).

Those who teach that all will be well in the end for everyone, make a mockery of life. I may struggle emotionally with hell, but even my limited sense of justice realises the necessity of judgment for those who have behaved monstrously in this life.

WHAT JESUS DIDN'T SAY

We would think it strange if a sports lover spent all their time focusing on rules and rules infraction. In the same way it is important that we get appropriate perspective when communicating the gospel. Yes, people need to know where their sin leads them, but this is only truly understood in its proper context. God is our Creator, sustainer, He sets the rules because of who He is, but makes our obedience to those rules possible. Judgment is a last resort and never vindictively executed. It is also great comfort that the world's evil will one day be dealt with. Without an understanding of God's judgment it is no surprise that people become discouraged and apathetic. Much of life would have no meaning if it weren't that God sees all things and will act.

MAIN POINTS

- Judgment is a necessary part of God's work and a theme that Jesus covers frequently.
- For some, the judgment of God will be terrible, they will face endless torment outside the presence of God.
- You will not come under condemnation as a believer in Jesus.
- If you serve God faithfully you will enjoy His reward.
- The theme of judgment, though sombre helps to make sense of an evil and corrupt world.

ACTION

1. With Christ's teaching about judgment in our minds, how can we do anything other than pray and act to help people know and understand the grace of God? Who do you need to pray for?

2. Thank Jesus that He took your punishment upon Himself.

Note

1. David L. Edwards and John Stott, *Evangelical Essentials: A Liberal–Evangelical Dialogue* (IVP, 1988.)

Chapter 29

It will be OK on that day

Coaching is often about helping people prepare for the future, so how great to have a Coach who knows the future. After all, the belief that a faith in Jesus will enable you to enter heaven is basic Christianity, isn't it? For many Christians, a faith in Jesus is largely about this future hope and if the concept of heaven is a bit hazy (and in many cases incorrect) it is still a real comfort. But Jesus never focuses on heaven as being the chief motive for following Him and the 'heaven' Christians are to enter is vastly different than many have imagined. We noted in Chapter 2 that Jesus calls us to a new kind of life. This is as much about where we spend the next ten minutes as where we spend eternity. Believers who have faith only for beyond death have missed a crucial dimension to Christianity and are destined for a pretty miserable life. The classic definition Jesus gives is that eternal life is to know Him and the Father (John 17:3). Knowledge is about relationship, it is about us getting to know Jesus better and better as we live under the rule and reign of God daily.

When the Pharisees asked Jesus when the kingdom of God would come, He replied: 'The kingdom of God does not come with your careful observation, nor will people say, "Here it is," or "There it is," because the kingdom of God is within you' (Luke 17:20–21). We have noticed elsewhere that this isn't the only thing Jesus says about the kingdom of God. Eternal life was to begin when we first repented of sin and trusted Christ and continues beyond the grave into the presence of God, awaiting the time when He will finally wind up this world. When people argue that Jesus talks more about hell than He does about heaven, they do Him a disservice. Yes, strictly speaking this may be true, but He speaks more about the kingdom than He does about hell. The kingdom has a now and a future dimension. Jesus knows that if you are in the kingdom now, the future takes care of itself.

Having noted the primary aspect of Jesus' teaching, what does He tell us about His future return?

Christ's return

Jesus was keen that His followers should grasp what He was planning. He told the Twelve that He was leaving to 'prepare a place' for them (John 14:1–3) and would return to take them to be with Him when God brings into being the eternal state – a new heaven and new earth where righteousness dwells. Given the momentous event it is no surprise that people have tried to search the Bible for clues as to when it might be. Perhaps the most important verse to notice is Jesus' clear statement that 'No-one knows about that day or hour, not even ... the Son ...' (Matt. 24:36). Jesus tells us that this decision is left to the Father. So speculation is futile; scholars and crystal-ball gazers cannot know.

But even if we can't locate the timing of Christ's return a number of things can be said about it. It will be:

(a) Personal
'... I will come again and will take you to myself, that where I am you may be also' (John 14:3, RSV). It is clear that Jesus Himself will come back. He is not sending angels, but will come personally in a way that will be recognisable.

(b) Sudden
Jesus said no one would know when it was and gave some examples of what might be happening when He returned: 'Two men will be in the field; one will be taken and the other left. Two women will be grinding

with a hand mill; one will be taken and the other left' (Matt. 24:40–41).

The coming will be out of the blue and welcomed by those who believe in Him who will join Him, though there is no indication in Scripture that the world will carry on as normal with people bemused or shocked by a sudden exit of believers.

(c) Spectacular
'They will see the Son of Man coming on the clouds of the sky, with power and great glory' (Matt. 24:30).

Contrast is often made between His two comings – the first noticed by a few shepherds and wise men, the second by the whole world.

Jesus tells us a series of parables to teach how we should prepare for His return.

1. Parable of the Marriage Feast: (Matt. 22:1–14; Luke 14:16–24)
   Lesson: Respond to the invite or you will miss out.
2. Parable of the Ten Virgins (Matt. 25:1–13)
   Lesson: Be prepared for His return. Don't assume it will never happen so that you leave God out of the equation.
3. The parables of the Talents and Minas (Matt. 25:14–30; Luke 19:11–27)
   Lesson: Keep using the talents God has given you. Your work here will determine the work you are given in the life to come.

What happens next?

The speculation surrounding the events following the Lord's return has filled many volumes, in particular speculation about six verses in Revelation 20, which speaks of believers reigning with Christ for 1,000 years. Some take this as indicating that Christ will set up a throne (in Jerusalem they say) for a literal 1,000 years and reign for that duration. Although this is not directly part of how the Twelve were coached by Christ, it does impact upon things He says to the Twelve. There are a number of reasons for questioning a literal 1,000-year reign:

1. Jesus never speaks of this.
2. The rest of Scripture does not suggest this will happen. There are references to the disciples reigning but these are best understood as speaking of life in the new heavens and new earth where, in new sinless bodies fitted for this new realm, we will enjoy the extraordinary renewed universe that God has planned.
3. Adherents to a millennial kingdom look at predictive passages in the Old Testament that don't seem to describe this world and conclude they must take place in their understanding of a millennial kingdom. They fail to realise that the final consummation of the kingdom of God (described also as the new heavens and new earth) is physical and that these descriptions can just as easily apply to the new heavens and earth.
4. None of the references to Christ's return connect it to a 'literal 1,000-year reign on earth'.

Thus it seems best to understand Revelation 20 as depicting Christ's ongoing reign over His kingdom in the Church age. Satan is bound during this period, as Jesus says in Matthew 12:25–29, though this does not mean he is not still active as we saw in Chapter 23. Apocalyptic language is often symbolic and so we can take 1,000 as indicative of the power and perfection of Christ's reign.

Heaven

If people are hazy and hesitant about hell, they are equally puzzled by heaven. Depictions of heaven as a place of clouds and harps and endless singing do not help and although most people know it's going to be good, they have little idea what it will be like.

The truth is that heaven (not to be confused with the kingdom of heaven in Matthew's Gospel) is vastly different from what most expect. I agree with many evangelical commentators who would say that it is a place where our soul is welcomed into God's presence, but is not our final resting place. It is like a waiting room until the new heavens and the new earth (the full consummation of the kingdom of God) finally comes into being. Jesus could say to the thief who was crucified alongside Him, 'Today you will be with me in paradise [heaven].' But He also spoke of returning to this world and coming into His kingdom (Matt. 24:30–31).

So when we die in Christ it is appropriate to say that 'we go to heaven'. We are in God's conscious presence. But when we think of eternity, we are better thinking of the new heavens and new earth – the consummation of the kingdom of God.

Some argue that God is 'outside time' and therefore when we die it is as if the world has ended. So if you die 50 years before the Lord's return you wake up as if it's 50 years later. But remember God created time. He is able to take good care of the saints who have gone before, who all await that glorious moment when Jesus returns as Judge and King.

The kingdom's final state

We have already noted that we enter the kingdom of God when we first follow Christ. Our next stage is heaven, where we enjoy the presence of God. In the final consummation of the kingdom after Christ's return, we will be given new bodies fitted with the new state.

Jesus tells us:

1. We will be there because of Jesus
   He said: '… I shall lose none of all that he has given me, but raise them up at the last day' (John 6:39).
2. Earthly relationships are transformed.
   There will be no marriage (Matt. 22:30).
3. We will be made glorious.
   'Then the righteous will shine like the sun in the kingdom of their Father' (Matt. 13:43).
4. We will enjoy the treasures stored up from our service (Matt. 6:20).
5. Jesus looked forward to it (Matt. 26:29).
6. It will include the worldwide gathering of believers (Luke 13:29).
   People will come from the north, south, east and west to the kingdom of God.

Many pictures of the life to come suggest an endless worship service, which may well be a turn off to you – I mean church is good, but eternally good? We won't experience death (John 8:51–52) – as we understand death – and according to Jesus' parable will be carried by angels to be with God (Luke 16:22). We will be intensely alive, knowing and understanding like never before. We will continue to be ourselves and be involved in reigning over the new heavens and earth with God, exploring, learning, having fun, travelling. Our human conception of these things are bound to underplay the glory – as Paul quotes Isaiah, 'No eye has seen, no ear has heard, no mind has conceived what God has prepared for those who love him' (1 Cor. 2:9).

WHAT JESUS DIDN'T SAY

The speculation concerning the return of Christ has generated considerable interest in some Christian communities. It is a good thing to read the Bible passages and come to a view. But some speculation has divided Christians unnecessarily. Many are obsessed with the Lord's return and speculate about the ways in which passages of Scripture are being fulfilled today, without spending energy helping others to get ready for the return, whenever it is.

MAIN POINTS

- Jesus tells you to live in the light of His return.
- Heaven is your resting place before He returns and brings in the new heavens and new earth.
- There is no geography of the new heavens and earth, but it will have some continuation with this world and it will be great.

ACTION

1. Spend some time looking at the passages in this chapter. If Jesus came today, would you be ready?
2. How can you get more excited about the prospect of the world to come?

Chapter 30

You don't need to find God's will, it was never lost

Christians expect Jesus to tell them what to do. Some want Him to tell them, some secretly fear He will mess up their life if they know what He wants; many more fear that they may have to do something they don't want with someone they don't like somewhere they don't want to be.

The questions they expect answers on are big ones. Where should they live? Who should they marry? What job should they do?

Questions about 'guidance', or 'knowing the will of God' have perplexed Christians down through the ages as they have grappled with taking the right path. Many people who address them from conference and church platforms seem to have God's number, and messages from Him on a daily basis. So when they face a big issue they wonder why God doesn't speak to them.

As you grow in your understanding of the new kind of life and grow in communication with Jesus, you will draw conclusions about changes you need to make in your life and discover the Coach's priorities. But there will be times when you will face a major decision and want to 'do the right thing'. What does our Coach advise?

When we look at the way Jesus coaches the disciples there is a complete absence of any apparent advice on these major areas.

There are very few occasions where Jesus specifically directs them. We don't hear Him telling the disciples to go to a particular town or village because they would be well received, nor is there any recorded direction to announce the kingdom to any particular individuals.

This fits with Jesus' own pattern of ministry. He had particular goals, as in Mark 1:38 where He chooses to continue preaching rather than heal because that was why He had come. He has the goal of reaching Jerusalem for His crucifixion, of course, and there were times when He chose to teach (Sermon on the Mount and Upper Room discourses), but most of the conversations and healings recorded seemed to come when people approached Him. But not only does Jesus not give specific direction, He doesn't seem to give the disciples particular tools for making decisions. There are no seminars entitled 'Finding the will of God', or specific direction on matters which they, and we today, might have regarded as vital.

All of which begs a number of questions about Jesus' teaching. Are we to conclude that the big matters of life are not important, or are we to view the area of guidance in a different way? Based on what He does say and what is implied, we can glean a number of things:

1. God's will is done, not found

On one occasion, Jesus' family are looking for Him. Word comes to Jesus, who uses the opportunity to say that 'Whoever does God's will is my brother and sister and mother' (Mark 3:34).

For Jesus, as with other Jews, God's will was revealed in the Old Testament Law. It was something you did. We have noted already that Jesus fulfils the Law completely Himself and calls us to live a new kind of life with Him where we obey His Word through the help of His Spirit. Life in the kingdom is about us doing what God wants. He calls us to an abundant life. A focus on what we regard as big issues (location, job, mate) at the expense of the character issues surrounding walking with Christ daily is to miss the point. If you lived with a grumpy old bore would it matter where you lived, what church you attended? Wouldn't you rather the grumpy bore became a joy to live with?

2. Learning from Jesus is our focus

Our priority in living is that we follow Jesus, learning to live the way He would live if He were us. At the heart of our walk is a surrendered will that says that we want God's way beyond all others and that we are prepared to give way when God directs our paths. Becoming a Christian means us choosing to repent of the old way of living and embrace God's new way, but we can be sure that there will be times when we re-visit this commitment when we find teaching we don't naturally like. The first question we need to ask when seeking guidance from God is, 'Am I prepared to do it when I know what He wants?'

3. Guidance doesn't avoid suffering

The first two points knock on the head any idea that we might avoid tough times if only we could make the right decisions. Some want God to guide them so they can be free from hassle and unpleasantness. Get me the right job, house, mate and all will be well. And if they face difficulty with any of these three (or other situations) they conclude that they must have 'got their guidance wrong'. It is true that we can make foolish moves and yes we want to avoid unnecessary unpleasantness, but the rest of Jesus' teaching leads us to expect times of hardship and difficulty, both because we are Christians in a hostile world and because we, and the world, are imperfect.

This prevents wasting unnecessary time and energy on thinking, 'If only I had taken a different course of action all would be well'. In most situations, and of course there will be exceptions, a decision one way or another will not make any difference to God's ability to work in our lives if we are committed to following His revealed will in the Bible.

4. God leaves some things up to us

Philosophers and theologians have spilt much ink upon the whole issue of the extent to which our will is truly free. They rightly note that our inherited rebellion against God prevents us from living as we should and that without God's help we are not free to choose the good we should choose.

But it does seem that Jesus takes our will and our wishes seriously. It is true that we abandon ourselves in favour of Christ, but this does not mean that we become spiritual zombies without wishes and feelings and desires. As a Christian, my will changes to be excited and invigorated by things that God loves and which, in this new kind of life, I am growing to love. So Jesus says, 'If anyone is thirsty let him come to me and drink.' He doesn't say, 'Thirst is inappropriate for a child of God.' Hence this extraordinary promise in John 15:7 that if you remain close to Christ you can ask for whatever you wish and it will be done.

Jesus is training us to want what He wants, not to grudgingly accept what He wants. There is no evidence in the teaching of Jesus that He has a blueprint that we have to wrestle out of Him. So often Jesus says to us that we are free to choose who to marry, where to live and work, which church to attend. He might say: 'I know you will want a partner that also loves Me and with whom you will enjoy companionship, so choose wisely, get to know him/her, see him/her in various contexts, see how you feel but use your head too.'

Before I joined *Christianity* magazine as Assistant Editor, I had two job offers – one from *Power* magazine, which would enable me to get back into a 'secular' job, something I was keen to do after eight years in Christian work and one from the Christian magazine. The salary was roughly the same. *Power* was closer to where I lived. Which should I choose? I had a weekend to decide. I agonised, prayed, chatted to a few close friends, prayed some more. But had no leaning either way. I chose *Christianity*, but can't say I had any indication one way or the other. Looking back I conclude that God was leaving me to decide. In the same way, choice of job, church, home, can all be made seeking God's wisdom and grace, asking the advice of friends and coming to a decision trusting that God will be with you wherever you decide to work and worship and with whom.

5. If specific direction comes, follow it

My scepticism of the idea that God has a blueprint for us to wrestle out of Him, does not mean I believe that God never indicates a particular course of action. Jesus did give specific direction to His disciples outside of teaching about character. The Twelve and the seventy were told what to take and what to say, even if they weren't given specific places to go. On the Mount of Transfiguration and in the Garden of Gethsemane Jesus told His closest friends to join Him. He told Peter that he would suffer the death of a martyr without saying where or when. After His resurrection He told His disciples to go ahead of Him to Galilee.

When Jesus taught His disciples prior to His departure, He explained that it was good that He was going away because He would send the Comforter (the Holy Spirit), literally, another just like Him. In the same way that Jesus gave specific direction on some occasions to His disciples, it is not surprising that the Holy Spirit will direct His people. Of course His primary work is enabling the character change as His followers obey His teaching, but there may be times when the Spirit gives specific direction. So if you have a major decision, then you are wise to talk to God about it. The mechanism whereby He gives direction varies. In Acts, when the apostles had the inner work of the Spirit, there were rare occasions when the disciples received dreams, visits from angels, words of prophecy.

They were also guided by an inner sense of compulsion that they had learned to recognise as the voice of God. Their study of the Scriptures was specifically applied to precise situations. We shouldn't be surprised if He guides us in the same way. If prayer is conversing with God about things that concern us both then we shouldn't be surprised if we find God giving us direction when we pray as we get to sense His inner leading. However, an absence of promptings needn't concern us either. I have had friends who have had prophecies, verses out of the blue and a sense of inner compulsion before making moves. And I have had friends who have made major moves because they 'fancied a change'. Both submitted their plans to God and He's big enough to bless both.

6. We trust in God to guide us

Jesus accepted the view of God depicted in the Old Testament that He is sovereign over the affairs of His people. In Proverbs 3:5-6 we read: 'Trust in the LORD with all your heart and lean not on your own understanding; in all your ways acknowledge him, and he will make your paths straight.' Jesus' view of His Father's work was big enough to believe that He was involved in our lives behind the scenes. As Paul would put it: '… in all things God works for the good of those who love him, who have been called according to his purpose' (Rom. 8:28).

So we can trust God, knowing that He will be in control, working for good as we learn from Him. There will be many occasions when we will make decisions that have massive ramifications, but have no idea at the time, maybe because we do not have the right facts to make the 'right' decision. If you look back, you may note how apparently haphazard events have had a profound affect on you: a teacher at school who inspired you, an illness, a friend you met, a job loss, a new job, and so on. Jesus taught His disciples to rest in the kingdom, allowing God to work things out and doing what He needs to do. For all our concern to make good and wise decisions, it reminds us that we shouldn't be so arrogant as to forget that we live for Him, and not the other way round.

7. We enjoy the future God has for us

Talk of guidance can be disabling. Maybe you can recall a time when anxiety about the next step coloured every waking moment. That's understandable and, for brief seasons, may be inevitable. But the new kind of life is different. Jesus asks whether we can add one moment to our lives through worry. Any time I focus on 'what's next' and believe me I have wasted hours on this myself, I forget to live for now and any time I worry about 'what's next' I stop putting my confidence in the One who will be with me in all my 'what nexts'.

What Jesus didn't say

As we have seen, Jesus doesn't promise specific direction for every decision we make. We can talk to Him about everything, conscious that He is coaching us so that we naturally choose the things that please Him. There will be times when He will give us specific direction, and when He does, we follow it, but often, maybe most of the time, He will have coached us to the point where we know what to do. We get on with it, enjoying the freedom of walking in the new kind of life He promises.

Main points

- Jesus coaches us to involve Him in our day-to-day lives and is developing us to make decisions in keeping with His purposes.
- Sometimes He intervenes to make a particular course of action clear.
- He is always at work behind the scenes helping us move forward with Him.
- You can relax and trust Him as you get on with the new kind of life you are living

Action

1. Reflect on the big decisions you have had to make. How sure were you that your decision was something God was happy with?
2. How has the view that God has a blueprint that we need to discover hindered believers? How would you advise someone who believes this?

Concluding remarks

Being coached by Christ is a process that will go on for the rest of our lives. As we learn to interact with Christ and as we face the seasons of life, we will find it a joy to learn from Him how to live the new kind of life that He offers.

But although there's always progress to be made we can rejoice in changes that are in place. We will find that natural reactions and patterns of behaviour are barely recognisable as we take on the character of Christ.

So, as you complete this book, be sure to have the vision of a 'new you' – strong.

Christ came that we might know life, life to the full. There's no reason why He would leave you out of His plans.

Give it all you can, and you can be sure that He will be right there with you.

andynicpeck@bigfoot.com

Acknowledgement

My thanks to Nick Page, Martin Saunders, John Buckeridge and Grace Benson who provided help and insight at various times; to the team at CWR who did a great editing job; and most of all to my wife Nic, for her support and ongoing encouragement.

Bibliography

PART ONE

France, R.T., *Jesus the Radical* (IVP, 1989).

John, J., *The Life* (Authentic Media, 2003).

Ortberg, John, *The Life You've Always Wanted* (Zondervan, 1997).

Stein, Robert H., *The Method and Message of Jesus' Teaching* (Westminster/John Knox Press, 1994).

Warren, Rick, *The Purpose-Driven Life* (Zondervan, 2002).

Willard, Dallas, *The Divine Conspiracy* (Zondervan, 1998).

PART TWO

Clark, Brent and Eldredge, John, *The Sacred Romance* (Nelson Books, 1997).

Lucas, Jeff, *How not to Pray* (Authentic Lifestyle, 2003).

Packer, J.I., *Keep in Step with the Spirit* (IVP, 1984).

White, John, *The Fight* (IVP, 1977).

PART THREE

Crabb, Larry, *Understanding People* (Zondervan, 1987).

Eldredge, John, *The Journey of Desire* (Nelson, 2000).

Piper, John, *Desiring God* (IVP, 1986).

Willard, Dallas, *Renovation of the Heart* (Navpress, 2002).

PART FOUR

Lewis, C.S., *Four Loves* (HarperCollins, 1960).

Ortberg, John, *Everybody's Normal Till You Get to Know Them* (Zondervan, 2003).

Warren, Rick, *Purpose-Driven Church* (Zondervan 1995).

PART FIVE

Boyd, Greg, *Is God to Blame?* (Kingsway, 2003).

Bubeck, Mark, *The Adversary* (Scripture Union, 1975).

Carson D.A., *How Long O Lord* (IVP, 1990).

Greene, Mark, *Thank God, It's Monday* (Scripture Union, 1999).

Hood, Neil, *God's wealth – Whose money is it anyway?*
(Authentic Lifestyle, 2004).

Johnstone, Patrick, *Operation World* (Authentic Lifestyle, 2001).

Manley Pippert, Beccy, *Out of the Saltshaker* (IVP, 1999).

Mittelberg, Mark, *Building a Contagious Church* (Zondervan, 2000).

Schneider, Floyd, *Friendship Evangelism* (Monarch, 1989).

Wenham, John, *The Enigma of Evil* (IVP, 1985).

PART SIX

David, Lawrence, *Heaven – It's not the end of the world*
(Scripture Union, 1995).

Robinson, Haddon, *Decision Making by the Book*
(Scripture Press, 1992).

Hoekema, A.A., *The Bible and the Future* (Paternoster, 1979).

Willard, Dallas, *Hearing God* (Zondervan, 1994).

National Distributors

UK: (and countries not listed below)
CWR, Waverley Abbey House, Waverley Lane, Farnham, Surrey GU9 8EP.
Tel: (01252) 784700 Outside UK (44) 1252 784700

AUSTRALIA: CMC Australasia, PO Box 519, Belmont, Victoria 3216.
Tel: (03) 5241 3288

CANADA: Cook Communications Ministries, PO Box 98, 55 Woodslee Avenue,
Paris, Ontario. Tel: 1800 263 2664

GHANA: Challenge Enterprises of Ghana, PO Box 5723, Accra.
Tel: (021) 222437/223249 Fax: (021) 226227

HONG KONG: Cross Communications Ltd, 1/F, 562A Nathan Road, Kowloon.
Tel: 2780 1188 Fax: 2770 6229

INDIA: Crystal Communications, 10-3-18/4/1, East Marredpalli, Secunderabad
- 500026, Andhra Pradesh. Tel/Fax: (040) 27737145

KENYA: Keswick Books and Gifts Ltd, PO Box 10242, Nairobi.
Tel: (02) 331692/226047 Fax: (02) 728557

MALAYSIA: Salvation Book Centre (M) Sdn Bhd, 23 Jalan SS 2/64,
47300 Petaling Jaya, Selangor.
Tel: (03) 78766411/78766797 Fax: (03) 78757066/78756360

NEW ZEALAND: CMC Australasia, PO Box 36015, Lower Hutt.
Tel: 0800 449 408 Fax: 0800 449 049

NIGERIA: FBFM, Helen Baugh House, 96 St Finbarr's College Road, Akoka, Lagos.
Tel: (01) 7747429/4700218/825775/827264

PHILIPPINES: OMF Literature Inc, 776 Boni Avenue, Mandaluyong City.
Tel: (02) 531 2183 Fax: (02) 531 1960

SINGAPORE: Armour Publishing Pte Ltd, Block 203A Henderson Road,
11-06 Henderson Industrial Park, Singapore 159546.
Tel: 6 276 9976 Fax: 6 276 7564

SOUTH AFRICA: Struik Christian Books, 80 MacKenzie Street,
PO Box 1144, Cape Town 8000.
Tel: (021) 462 4360 Fax: (021) 461 3612

SRI LANKA: Christombu Books, 27 Hospital Street, Colombo 1.
Tel: (01) 433142/328909

TANZANIA: CLC Christian Book Centre, PO Box 1384, Mkwepu Street, Dar es
Salaam.
Tel/Fax: (022) 2119439

USA: Cook Communications Ministries, PO Box 98, 55 Woodslee Avenue, Paris,
Ontario, Canada.
Tel: 1800 263 2664

ZIMBABWE: Word of Life Books, Shop 4, Memorial Building,
35 S Machel Avenue, Harare.
Tel: (04) 781305 Fax: (04) 774739

For email addresses, visit the CWR website: www.cwr.org.uk
CWR is a registered charity - number 294387

Day and Residential Courses

Counselling Training

Leadership Development

Biblical Study Courses

Regional Seminars

Ministry to Women

Daily Devotionals

Books and Videos

Conference Centre

Trusted all Over the World

CWR HAS GAINED A WORLDWIDE reputation as a centre of excellence for Bible-based training and resources. From our headquarters at Waverley Abbey House, Farnham, England, we have been serving God's people for 40 years with a vision to help apply God's Word to everyday life and relationships. The daily devotional *Every Day with Jesus* is read by over three-quarters of a million people in more than 150 countries, and our unique courses in biblical studies and pastoral care are respected all over the world. Waverley Abbey House provides a conference centre in a tranquil setting.

For free brochures on our seminars and courses, conference facilities, or a catalogue of CWR resources, please contact us at the following address. CWR, Waverley Abbey House, Waverley Lane, Farnham, Surrey GU9 8EP, UK

Telephone: **+44 (0)1252 784700**
Email: **mail@cwr.org.uk**
Website: **www.cwr.org.uk**

CRUSADE FOR WORLD REVIVAL
Applying God's Word to everyday life and relationships

Christ Empowered Living
Selwyn Hughes

Christ Empowered Living is Selwyn Hughes' dynamic core
teaching in one easy to digest volume.

It will transform your life with essential principles of
Christian living and develop you to your full spiritual potential.
You will discover biblical insights that will revolutionise your
approach to the way you live and help to renew your mind.

This latest edition improves readability and gives larger
margins for notes.

ISBN: 1-85345-201-7

£7.99 (plus p&p)

The 7 Laws of Spiritual Success
Selwyn Hughes

Just as there are laws in nature that hold our physical world
together, so there are laws for life that make our spiritual
walk a success. This book is Selwyn Hughes' legacy to future
generations and esstential reading for anyone who has been
inspired by his teaching and ability to apply God's Word to
everyday life and relationships.

ISBN: 1-85345-237-8

£7.99 (plus p&p)

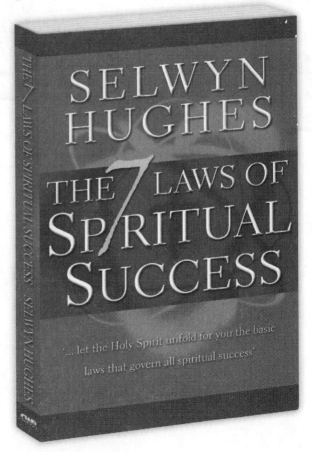

Your Personal Encourager
Selwyn Hughes

The revised edition of *Your Personal Encourager* presents a
new design for a classic bestseller that will show you how to
encourage yourself and others in God. With more than four
decades of counselling experience Selwyn Hughes deals with
40 of life's most common problems, including fear,
disappointment and bereavement, simply and effectively.
Topics include: When God seems far away, When hopes are
dashed, When doubts assail.

ISBN: 1-85345-072-3

£4.99 (plus p&p)

OVER 100,000 COPIES SOLD IN 7 LANGUAGES

Your
Personal
Encourager

BIBLICAL HELP FOR DEALING
WITH DIFFICULT TIMES

Selwyn Hughes

Prices correct at the time of printing.